Lawrence Edward West

The Life of a
Good Ole Country Boy

International Standard Book Number 0-87012-770-5
Library of Congress Control Number 2008900417
Printed in the United States of America
Copyright © 2008 by Lawrence West
Beeson, WV
All Rights Reserved
2008

As I begin this story, I have never written one before, but as I attempt to write this one, I will try my best to bring out the life and history of this good ole country boy. I believe in history and I will try to be as accurate as I can be. I think we should document the memories of those we have lived among, after all they keep records of our presidents, that have all been carried high after they leave their offices, and all of the elected officials who have authority over us, so you might agree with me about some of these old timers, as they maybe more important to some of us than the past elected officials. These old timers were down to earth people; you see these people worked hard with long hours. After their work day had finished, they had to walk seven or eight miles and some of them even more to get home. They had to get up the next morning and do the same thing over and I can't understand for the life of me how they held up with no more sleep than they got at night. Now you see men and women were the salt of the earth, just the way that Jesus spoke to his disciple. These were men and women we should be happy that we knew. I am glad that my wife and I were here to take part in all this history; Even though she has passed and gone on now, I am glad that I have played a part in this. This good ole country boy has been blessed while growing up in Beeson, West Virginia.

I am going to write about the people that my wife and I had the good pleasure of knowing and seeing as we grew up here. There were some good people here in Beeson, West Virginia. We have seen them and talked with them but now most of them have passed and gone on, along with my dear wife. I believe this is not the end, I believe if we trust in the Lord, we will meet again, somewhere over in paradise.

I will write a lot of things about people I have known, things I have seen and heard. I have many memories about people I loved and trusted. That's the reason I can call myself a Good Ole Country Boy. I know there are a lot of other good ole country boys, if they would just tell about the memories that they had. These old timers are history, and we can honor them although they have departed this life.

I was born in a little town named Matoaka, West Virginia. It was a small town, and brother it was a booming little town. The mining companies had moved in early on. If I remember correctly, there were five or six big coal companies. They had a lot of employee's at that time; they didn't have any big machines in those days, all the work had to be done by hands, picks, and shovels.

I can remember the company store. They had anything you would want. The miners would buy the things they needed and the company would hold it out of their check. I recall one man that had bought a box of cheerios and ice cream. He said if he had known that it was that good, he would have bought a chop sack full.

Now the little town of Matoaka that I was born in had a lot of stores and I was told it was named after an Indian. I just don't know for sure, I'd say there might be one or two still living that could tell about it. That was many years ago. The place was prosperous, I do know that much. There were two car dealerships; one was a Ford dealership and the other a Chevy dealership. I'm thinking they had the franchise for both garages. There was a chicken hatchery, and I am uncertain of the number of grocery stores. There were two or three gasoline stations, a five and ten cent store, a shoe shop, a dry goods store, and several restaurants and beer joints. I remember one time, a friend of mine had told me of a family that had gone into town, and the man's name was Charlie. His wife had gone to do her shopping, when she finished she couldn't find Charlie anywhere. You see, Charlie was a little like Zaccheus in the Bible, but Zaccheus may have been a better man than Charlie was. Finally, Charlie's wife found him in a beer joint, sitting between two women, drinking beer. She said come on Charlie, let's go home and she left the building. Well Charlie never did come, so she went back into the beer joint and he is still sitting at the same ole place, so she reached over and nabbed him by the shirt collar and said, come on Charlie let's go. Charlie replied, alright, I'll go, but I don't want to.

Also in the town of Matoaka there was a jewelry store, two or three dentist offices, about three doctors' offices, a drug store, theater, bank, funeral home and two taxi stands, I believe there were three taxi cabs in each company. They would stay busy all day and night on Friday's, and Saturday's. There were two train depots, one was the Virginia Railroad and the other was North and Western Railroad. There was a Post Office and up in the holler there was a skating ring. There were two schools; the larger school was located on top of a mountain. This mountain was called school house hill. The right hand side of the hill was named Thompson Hill, and another mountain was called Carter Hill, and yet another mountain was named Grave Yard Hill. You had to cross two railroad tracks to get to the top of Grave Yard Hill. I can see right now that I have already lost some of you people, but you see that is what it takes to be a Good Ole Country Boy.

I had a conversation with a Mr. Davis and his wife; in fact I visited their home. They were very gracious with me; they have a good recollection of things that happened in the town. The pictures that they had were amazing to look at. Looking back in time, Mr. Davis believes the town of Matoaka took its name in 1901. He also told me of things of another place approximately one mile above Matoaka. I knew about this place, but Mr. Davis says this town had about five stores. This place was/is called Giato, West Virginia. I knew it had a beer joint. Mostly all blacks lived there. This place was a knock down and carry out place. I was once told that when the snow would fall on the weekend, blood would get in the snow and it was nick-named blood city. I used to go there with my grandmother when she would peddle her milk, eggs, and garden food in the summer. Grandmother took the milk and eggs year round. I don't remember who the gentleman was, but he said that someone had cut the back of his belt in two pieces, I will tell you right now that was a call. He was down there at the beer joint in Giato, West Virginia, the place I was talking about that was a knock down drag out. Some people may say I have no business talking about black people. We lived here in Beeson; some of the black people would come and visit on Sunday's. I don't remember their names, but they were all dressed to the top. You would have thought that the gentleman had come to preach. Now all this stuff I have written about is history from my point of view. I still believe that history should be left from some person in each community. In the years to come, those people will never know that we existed. I was talking about the black people, we are all God's creatures and we are probably all made from the same batch of mud.

My Dad
Reverend
Roger West

My Dad's name was Roger West; he
worked in and around the mines. He
worked outside on the tipple. This is
where they washed the coal off and
screened it for shipment. My
grandfather also worked in the mines,
where they would lay cinders and hang
curtains to turn the air in different
directions, so they would have the right
ventilation for the miners who were

working inside the mines.

At the coal mines where Dad worked, there was a bath house, where they would change into their work clothes. In the winter time, the homeless would go there and lay on the benches, so they could stay warm throughout the night. The coal miners didn't have room to sit down to put their shoes on. All of the men got together one day to try and figure out how to get rid of these men. They came up with a plan, or maybe the better word would be a scheme to get rid of these men. A day or two later they began to carry out their scheme. Two of the men got into a fight, and one of them began to run. As he ran to the front door, the other man shot him (the gun had blank bullets). The homeless men came off of the benches and started running across the man lying at the door, needless to say, they didn't come back. As you can see, the scheme worked.

My Mother
Myrtle Blankenship West,
Lawrence West,
Eilene West, Christine West

My mother, Myrtle Blankenship West,
Lawrence West,
Eilean West, and
Christine West

My mother was a Blankenship; her name was Myrtle; she was raised on a mountain top called Nubbins Ridge. Nubbins Ridge is where I later found the love of my life. My mother's parents lived there on a little farm. My grandfather Blankenship ran a little grocery store on Nubbins Ridge. I never knew of my Grandfather Blankenship working anywhere on public works. Now that tells me something about him, but that doesn't keep me from being a good ole country boy. My wife's family was next door neighbors to my grandparents, if you can call a quarter of a mile neighbors. My maternal grandmother was a good ole soul; she was a hard working lady and raised a large family. I believe she also raised four grandchildren.

12

Myrtle West
My Mother

Now I will tell you a little about the things that happened as Beeson, West Virginia became a small community and the band saw business began. Before Beeson, this community was called Hardwood; I have been told that Beeson was named after a family that lived here. A family came to my house from the state of Georgia that confirmed the things that have been told. They told me that when change came here, there was a family by the name of Beeson's that lived here. I will tell you the year in which all of this took place, in nineteen and thirteen it had taken the name of Hardwood. I presume there was nothing there but mountains and trees. Therefore I believe that was when the band saw mill was brought in. In nineteen hundred and Fourteen a man named Earl O'Harrah became the post master and although I am not for sure I think he also owned the saw mill. He was the post master from 1914 till March 12th 1917. On October 12th 1917, Mr. Otha Burton took the Post Office until October 16th in the year of 1944. Then Mrs. Lydia Rose took over as post master, she remained there until

October 31st, 1959, then my wife Faye West took the post master position which she kept until she retired in 1997. At this time they closed the post offices and put in NDCBV boxes on my (Lawrence West) property, so the community could get their mail and it would be safe, each person had their own key. Now people this may not turn your red flag up or down. But this is history that I am writing about, and it makes me feel good knowing that my wife was part of this history. My wife has already passed on, and now you can see how I have been blessed as a Good Ole Country Boy.

Before my time, there was a band mill here in Beeson. They would build small roads across or around the mountain and tram their logs to the band mill with Dinks. My Grandfather West ran one of the dinks. They would take their sawed lumber to Springton, West Virginia to load on railroad cars. I was told they used a horse and buggy to deliver the lumber.

Dinky

Work Horses and men hauling out
timber

Roger and Myrtle West

My Dad and Mother moved from Matoaka to Beeson, when I was around two years old, or less. They found a little flat spot of land around a hillside, about a quarter of a mile from the country road. They used a horse and sled to haul lumber on. They built a three room house; there was a little spring on the side of the country road from there, and we had to carry water to drink. Dad had to make a road, from the little three room house to the country road. One of my uncles on my mother's side of the family was a school teacher, and my other uncles were top notch carpenters. I don't know where I was when all of those talents were handed out, I must have been misplaced somewhere, but you know, that didn't keep me from being a Good Ole Country Boy.

I was four years and five months old when my mother passed away. Prior to her death she had given birth to, my two sisters Christine and Ileane then later on mom gave birth to a little baby boy. The birth of my little brother is how my mother was taken from me. Before they took my mother to the hospital, she hugged my sisters, told them to be good and to mind their grandmother, I then went to her bedside, she told me to help my grandmother with my sisters, and to mind my grandmother and grandfather. That day we didn't know we would never see our mother and brother alive again. Those words that my mother spoke have never left my mind. Folks, if you have a mother, father, brother or sister, love them with all your heart. You see, when my mother left that room going to the hospital; that was the end of the hugs and kisses. My mother had a rough life. When my dad would come in from work, the war was on. Over next to the country road, there was a big tree stump, I would guess that it was at least three feet across, my mother would sit on that stump, hug my sisters and I up close to her and cry for hours. I don't think my dad ever knew that I remembered these events. When someone mistreats your mother, it's hard to forget. It laid out a plan for me, to never mistreat my wife. If my wife was still living today, she would say this is true. Our mother passed from this life on February eighth, 1936, in the winter months. There was lots of snow; it was like a blizzard that day. I thought that I could remember my Grandpaw West, taking my two sisters on a horse, but some say it was my Grandmother West on the horse, and that some of the neighbors had kept my sisters at home. I just don't know. But one thing I do know is that my Grandfather West's neighbor Mr. Shrewsbury took me on one of his horses. Mr. Shrewsbury and I were talking about that day, and he told me there was no way I could remember that day, because I was too young. I began to tell him of things that had happened that day and he agreed that I did remember. To cap the stacks, our Great Grandmother and Great Grandfather were buried the following week. They were killed by their son-in-law in the town of Matoaka.

I wasn't old enough to remember my Great Grandfather Reverend John Wyatt and my Great Grandmother. I only saw them once or twice; I was always told that he was a preacher. One of my Uncles had told me that he and my Aunt Beulah talked about why I

didn't sing for my Great Grandfather,
his family was thought to be the best
singers around, and I believe they sang
acapella style. I obtained a copy of
their funeral and it was said that
George Hager; the little boy that he had
was thirteen years old and was with
them when they were killed on
February Fifteenth Nineteen Hundred
Thirty Six. My Great Grandparents
were well liked by everyone at that
time and age.

John and Virginia Wyatt
My Grandparents

Bluefield Daily Telegraph. Bluefield, WV
February 15 1936

Matoaka Pastor Indicts State
For Rum-crazed Dual Murder

The Rev. R.O. Eller Scores Sales Of Legalized Liquor
In Sermon At Joint Funeral Services For Mr. And
Mrs. John Wyatt, Slain By Son-In-Law

The state of West Virginia was held by the Rev. R. O. Eller, pastor of the Matoaka Methodist Church. directly responsible for the brutal murder of the Rev. John Wyatt, 79, and his wife, Mrs. Virginia Wyatt, 77, who were shot to death by their son-in-law, George Hager, 39, at their home in Matoaka on the evening of February 15.

In one of the most unusual and sensational funeral sermons ever delivered, the Methodist minister brought one of the bitterest indictments against the state of West Virginia and legalized liquor that has ever been made from the pulpit in this section.

The tragic death of the aged couple and the suicide of their assassin came as a climax to a long fight which the church people of Matoaka have been waging against the West Virginia Liquor Control commission to prevent them from establishing a liquor dispensary in Matoaka. Twice the commission has been enjoined.

Crowd Auditorium

Approximately 900 people, who crowded into the auditorium of Matoaka high school last Monday afternoon to attend the joint services for Mr. and Mrs. Wyatt, heard the Rev. Mr. Eller bring the indictment against the state.

Holding in his hand the bottle of, half-filled with liquor, which had been taken from the person of George Hager, the Methodist minister, in a very dramatic manner, exclaimed "I hold in my hand the bottle half-full from which George Hager drank the damnable liquor bought from a licensed liquor store, which sent him to the accomplishment of his hellish purpose."

"They (the liquor crowd) have told you to put the seal of the state on a bottle of liquor will turn it into a Sunday school But there lies before us today the evidence of what it will do, regardless of what seal is on it. You on the front entrance. *This bottle says the contents are 100-proof. That is right. The contents of this bottle were 100 percent effective, three murders two broken homes, twenty orphans, one hundred broken hearts in one-half the contents. Double that and you have the meaning of the sign on the bottle, 100-proof. Why not put the proper sign on every bottle of the damnable stuff, the skull and crossbones, as you do on any other poison Why not write under that sign, "The man who drinks the contents of this bottle shall not only die. but kill every body with whom he comes in contact."*

My friends, let me construct for you another side of this sad picture George Hager had been suddenly turned into a foul murderer by the influence of intoxicating liquor. He has committed one of the vilest crimes of human history. But that does not change the fact that he was somebody's father, just the same. That night about dark , as he lay dying like a dog on the back porch of this ill-fated house, a little boy (13-years) appeared over the little river separating the house from the town proper, and inquired where his father was laying. They told him he was dying. The little boy exclaimed , "Is anybody doing anything for him?" When told his father was receiving no attention, the little boy cried, "Why don't somebody help my daddy?" The state of West Virginia has not enough money to repair the damage done in that child's heart. His daddy died that night just after mid-night in a hospital in Princeton. where in answer to the boy's prayer the police took him.

The state of West Virginia has just finished making a half-million dollars from the sale of the stuff that killed these two good old people. Where, I ask you, did the state get the money? They got it from hungry mouths and shivering and the wives of the men they sent to jail for the use of this state agent and widows and orphans of those who have already speckled the hills of the state with their graves from the use of legal liquor. Where can the state best spend this money? I am no politician. Nor am I an authority on finance. But any right thinking citizen of this or any other state can tell them the only place left to spend this money, the only place there is left to spend this money, the only place they can afford to spend it. Let the state buy a large tract of land on one of West Virginia's scenic hills or mountains and there erect a beautiful orphan's home left in the wake of this wholesale carnage in following the great flow of liquor from the state. But no, they will never do that. These children and loved ones will be left at the mercy of a cold-blooded. heartless world with no one save the church and God to love them

Suppose you could take that "Famous check for a half million dollars--- that check hailed so loudly by the wet press of this state, and cash it into one dollar bills and carpet the path to place of mourning. this morning. Suppose each child and grand-child could, this morning. have walked on

can no more change the contents of a bottle of liquor by the seal on it than to change Hell by hanging the picture of Jesus Christ on the front entrance.

Broken Hearts

In the course of his remarks, the minister paused to point out that the act committed by Hager, for which he held liquor responsible, had only left in its wake broken hearts in the Wyatt family, but also in Hager's family. The pathetic plight of George Hager's thirteen-year old son was vividly described in a very touching and impressive manner. "The state of West Virginia has not enough money to repair the damage done in that child's heart," the minister declared.

The complete text of Mr. Eller's sermon follows:

Friends, we stand this morning in the presence of the saddest tragedy of the century in our community, or the nation. It would be impossible to imagine a sadder one any where or any time. A Baptist preacher, 79, and his life-long companion, 77, brutally and foully murdered by a drunken assassin in the state of West Virginia, by a citizen of the same state, drunken on the liquor sold him by said state. This crime shall ever remain a black spot on this state which sold him the liquor that drove him to this most heinous crime.

On February 15, 1936, about five-thirty, these two good old-fashioned people sat in the evening glow of life with their family about them, enjoying the place they called home, when the assassin entered and left them and himself dead in the four walls that kept them, and under the roof that sheltered them from winter's withering blasts. Two better and more innocent people never lived in this community. They had harmed no man. Their lives were taken from them as a direct result or West Virginia state-owned, state-sold, and state-sealed, 100-proof liquor. I hold in my hand the bottle half-full, from which George Hager drank the damnable liquor, bought from a licensed liquor store, which sent him to the accomplishment of his hellish purpose.

They (the liquor crowd) have told you to put the seal of the state on a bottle of liquor will turn it into a Sunday school. But there lies before us today the evidence of what it will do, regardless of what seal is on it. You may add to this seal contained on this bottle (West Virginia Liquor Control Commission) the seal of the United States, the picture of Jesus and Heaven, the sun and moon and stars, and it still contains the very dregs of Hell Fire in its hellish contents. very dregs of Hell Fire in its hellish contents. You can no more change the contents of a bottle of liquor by the seal on it than you can change Hell by hanging the picture of Jesus Christ this veritable carpet of fabulous money. That carpet could not have eraced one picture from their mind nor have healed one ache in the heart of a friend.

Suppose the state shall erect this orphan's home. Suppose they build a palatial mansion for the care of those who follow the black wagon to the West Virginia hills. Suppose they floor every room with marble, build every mantle with the finest ivory, make every window sill of pure gold and every window frame of unadulterated silver, every glass from rose-tinted art glass, and stud them with the costliest gems from the mines and ocean depths of earth to mellow the sunshine as it falls on the golden hair and sparkling eyes of those left to this sad fate; not one picture could ever be eradicated nor one pain of despair be removed.

But, alas, and alas, not, not so. These shall be left to the care of the so much hated and abused Christian Church. The task shall fall in the hands of narrow-minded biggots and hair-brained fanatics they call church members. If that is what they are, then, friends, let us continue to be until this damnable liquor traffic shall end.

Beeson, West Virginia was a good place to grow up in. There was a good atmosphere to grow up in. As I look back at my life after being seventy-five years old I can say its good being a good ole country boy. I have been blessed beyond compare. Growing up I was raised on a one horse farm, we would plant corn on the hillside. When it came time to hoe the corn, it would seem as if we would never get to the other end. Up in the day, we would wonder when dinner time would come, and brother it was hot in those days. These days they talk about global warming, some of those people should have been around in those days, if they had been, they would think differently. Getting back to the corn field, my grand-paw (that's what I called him) would plow the corn out with a horse and plow, then, my Aunt Vernie and I would hoe the corn. My Aunt Vernie was only four years older than I. We were more like brothers and sisters; she and I worked as a team. I remember one time we sat down to rest under a shade tree and a scorpion went up my pants leg; now brother, you talk about someone doing a war dance, I was preparing to undress and leave there. There are so many things to think about growing up. After being in the fields all day, Grandmaw would make us go out to the branch to wash our feet, before we could go to bed. We would get up on the hillside and mow the grass. After it dried, we would have to go to the top of the hill and take a pitch fork and roll the dried grass down to the bottom, then carry it to the barn. I can recall seeing my uncle George West down the road from our home throwing rocks at a hornets nest. The nest was way up in a tree, he wasn't having any luck at knocking it out. About this time Garland came along. Garland said he could knock it off of that limb, so he threw a few rocks, and wasn't having any luck either. He then decided to go down the road to get a little closer. Almost straight under the nest, he then threw a rock, and down the nest came. A bunch of hornets were after him and some of the bees stung him. George began to laugh at Garland, because he said that he wouldn't get stung, but those bees took a near cut on him. Garland was the man who ate all the apple pies, which I will tell you about later on.

As a small country boy being raised in a small community, everybody loved you and you loved everybody. You couldn't come into Beeson West Virginia without being loved, or loving someone when you left. There were a lot of elderly people there, and I can remember a lot of the things they have said. I was blessed to be raised in Beeson. You could whisper and no-one would hear, or if they did hear what you said, they wouldn't tell anyone else. Isn't that great; you couldn't do that in New York City. Isn't it great being a good ole country boy in these hills and valley's, in almost heaven, West Virginia. You can't beat that with a ten foot pole, but if you could you would have to watch that ten foot pole, because some of these old mountain men may come up behind you and whittle your ten foot pole down to their size, and that's what makes it great being a good ole country boy. It's wonderful being a country boy, I would go down to the creek and see those beautiful butterflies and all the different colors, and I could watch the honey bees drinking. You could see the old timers come by the creek, to watch the bees. They would watch the course in which they would fly; they would follow the bees to find out which tree their hive was in. The old timers would then put their name on the tree so that later in the fall they would go and cut down the tree, so they could get the honey. Some of the honey would be clear and some would be dark. The color depends on the bloom the bees had worked. That's what it takes to be a Good Ole Country Boy.

As a young boy, growing up in these West Virginia hills, we were able to see a lot of things that young people in the city never had the opportunity to see. We never had the bright lights that high lighted the city boy's life. But as a country boy, I had the opportunity to take a stroll in the woods everyday, and enjoy all of the wondrous things that God had made. The birds would get high in the trees and sing. It is wonderful to see and hear the squirrels, and watch them jump from limb to limb. They would stop and bark then go again. I could watch the old groundhog run down the road and back into his hole in the ground. I would watch the deer running through the woods with their white flag raised in the air, and the raccoons waddle out of sight. We can look over the hills and it reminds us of what the Lord said; he owns the cattle on a thousand hills, as we go over all these things, it reminds us of all the things he has put on this earth for us to look at and to enjoy.

When I was a young lad, we would go into the woods and cut a grape vine.

We would swing across the hollow and back again. Someone would give us a push and here we would go. It was lots of fun being a Good Ole Country Boy.

Grandpa & Grandma Blankenship

Christine   Eilean   Lawrence

Christine West   Eilean West

My grandparents were good to me and my sisters. Our dad had gotten married again, her name was Hettie. In earlier years, my dad was a wicked man. I am not for sure but I was told that they went somewhere in Tennessee to get married. Together they had five children; three girls and two boys. Once they had come to get us and our clothes. They lived about a fourth of a mile from Grandpa's house. I was to sleep in the back room, but when dark would fall, I would slip out the back window and go back to Grandpa's house. That's where we wanted to be. The next day I would take a wheel barrel and go back to my Dad's house to get my sisters and our clothes. That same evening, they would come back again to get us and our clothes. When dark fell, the same thing would happen again. I don't know exactly how long this went on, until one evening, they came for us and my Grand paw told them to go on and leave us alone. Now this was what my sisters and I wanted to hear.

A while after my two sisters and I went to live with our grandparents. In the summer months, my sisters and I would watch for our grandfather to come home from work. We wanted to see if he had any sandwiches in his bucket. He would have one or two left over from his lunch, and he would hand his bucket over to us. We divided the sandwiches between us and those sandwiches were good after being many miles under the mountains. I believe granddad enjoyed all this as much as we did. Once I was running around in the grass fields and I heard a sound that I had never heard before. It had me a little bit scared, and after a bit I got enough nerve to go see what it was. I waited there until granddad came over to see, and it was a blowing viper snake.

My sisters and I were blessed. We had clothes to wear, a roof over our heads and we had plenty to eat. When our Grandma spoke, you had better take heed. When she said; I'm going to whip you, you better believe that she was. Many times I would lie on the horse sled until the early morning, when I thought that everyone was asleep. I would go into the house and get in the bed, and then here Grandma would come with a switch. Now brother, that wasn't very pleasant on my legs. When it was time to get out of bed, Grandma would come to the door and yell, and you had better get out of the bed or here she would come with a big cup of water. She would throw the water right in my face and that wasn't very pleasant either, because it was winter time and that old house was cold anyway.

We lived up in a hollow; there was our family and one other family. I believe the weather has changed, because back in the late thirties and all of the forty's, there was a creek that ran in front of our house. In the spring, and all thru the summer, we would go out on the front porch and listen to the frogs holler and sometimes we could hear the whippoorwills. There was such a warm breeze that came down the hollow. After seventy years, that warm breeze doesn't come thru like it used to. I now live within a mile of the old home place. Back then the old owls would hoot and hoot. Now you talk about an ole country boy living in the good ole days, I was one of them.

Lawrence West

When I was six years old, I started to school. The school was a two room building. One room was for grades one thru four, and the other room was for grades five thru eight. From the ninth grade on we had to go to Matoaka High School. We had to ride a bus to Matoaka. The bus ran at seven o'clock am. We would have to walk a mile to catch the bus. Before going to school we had to eat breakfast and feed the live stock. Now some say those were the good ole days, but you can't prove that by me. Now I am reminded of the years that all the young people in the community would head back to school and that would be the day after Labor Day. Some of the children would be happy to be back to school with their friends and some of us wouldn't. Even though we were young lads we can all say it was a joyful experience, and maybe, just maybe we might have brought something away from this little two room school that helped some of us to succeed in life. Some of the children went on to be successful in life after they got out of high school and some of us didn't amount to a handful of peas. I'm talking about myself now. Well now that's enough about that. While we were there in that one room, we looked forward to recess and going home time. One of the games we would play at recess was crack the whip. There would

be fifteen or twenty children and
brother the one on the end was in for a
treat; and sometimes we played auntie
over; Which was throwing the ball over
the school house. Before someone threw
the ball they would holler auntie over;
Sometimes, we would play soft ball
behind the school house. There was
another school in Pinoak, West
Virginia; we would get together and
play ball. Both schools would get
together and each school would take
half a day off and we all had a
wonderful time. Now at the end of the
school year our school would go on a
picnic and most of the time we would
go to the West hollow as the people at
school called it. I don't know why they
called the hollow by that name. There
was another family of Shrewsbury's
and they were good neighbors and they
were a hard working family. Now this
Mr. Shrewsbury had a ton or a ton and
half truck. Sometimes he would have
the cattle racks on and he would take
the school kids to a place called
fountain park, here in West Virginia;
They also had a skating ring and at the
end of the day when we left there were
some sore rear ends. Now that was a
part of being (a good ole country boy).
I remember one time I was in the fifth
grade up to the eighth grade class
room; I called the teacher's name
Robert. One day two drunks came along

and they were trying to take the teacher's car and he went to see what they were trying to do. They ran him back into the school house; I don't know how many times one of the men chased Mr. Robert around the room. One of the students got up in the aisle and the drunk got him by the hair of his head. He picked him up and threw him out of the way. Then they went down to one of the neighbor's houses and picked up a jug of kerosene. I don't think he drank too much. As I remember he spent the night there and I don't remember where the other man went. One time the people in the community got up a play, I don't know if any of them wrote the play or they got it some place. They had the play at our school. You know that was a big thing in our community because we didn't have anything for entertainment and all the people turned out to see it. The play was quite comical and it was well received by all the people in our community. For me as a young lad I can remember a girl going to the dentist once. She was holding the side of her head, groaning with her tooth. The dentist set her in a chair. He got his tools out to work with, and then he went to work on his patient. She was groaning something awful and he pulled a wooden tooth out of her mouth. I would say it was an inch or inch and half long. I think her dad whittled the tooth out, now isn't it nice living the life of a Good Ole Country Boy.

You see when I was a young lad I would visit all of these older people. I went back and forth at times, I would tell people, that they would say; Maybe he is a little old red headed boy just roaming through the community without a home or a family. This is all hog wash about this and could be called a lie but it's mine and I can tell it any way I want to. But the beauty of this is I loved all of these old people of course. I have let it be known all along in this writing. By now you know I just love old people, how about you?

We had to start to work at an early age, something like the age of six. My Grand-Parents believed that if you were big enough to carry a goose neck hoe, that you were big enough to use it. You know this didn't cotton so well with this poor little ole country boy. There was a bunch of us in that little old house. Right off hand, I don't exactly remember how many there were, but there was a bunch. Most of the time, there was one old Grandpa, two old Grandmas, Uncles and Aunts; and there were Grandkids all the time, sometimes as many as six or seven Grandkids. It was rough in those days. If there was any meat at our house, they would make it go as far as it would go. They would cut off about an inch square and boil it. They would then run a string thru the meat and tie a big knot on one end, then they would tie the other end to the ceiling. There was a little step ladder you had to step on to get a piece of meat, then you would climb down and another would go up the ladder for their piece of meat. Each and everyone would get the same amount of nourishment. Well, ha ha I just got carried away a little bit. It wasn't all that bad. The truth is that at Grandma's house, she had a big long table in the dining room, and when the meal was ready, the table was full. This is why I was Grandma's boy. By now you can see that I was blessed.

As I grew up in Beeson West Virginia, we didn't have many fancy things where we lived. The most fancy thing we had was the outhouse and the sears catalog. Brother let me tell you, when you have to get up in the middle of the night to go to the bathroom and you have to tread out in a foot of snow, in zero degree weather; that's just part of being a Good Ole Country Boy. I've always wondered why they put the outhouse in the house.

We had some awful roads here in Beeson. There was mud everywhere. There were ruts in the roads that were really deep. Back in those days, people would split rails out of wood to make fences. They would have their fences looking really nice, then someone would come along and take their fence rails and put them in the deep ruts in the road. We lived under a mountain and it was about a mile up the hollow to our house. It was really rough trying to get a car in there in the winter time. It was around Nineteen Hundred Fifty before we got a hard top road. It was about this time that we also got electricity. We used to sit around the dining room table doing our homework by an oil lamp. We could spot a flea sitting on the flour barrel. Now since we have electricity we can't see a big elephant in the room; oh my how things have changed. They tell me how some things, like whiskey would get better and taste better after it had aged. Well I don't think that has worked for me.

As a boy, we would work in the garden as I mentioned earlier. I was seven or eight years old, and I would plow the garden. I would have to stand on a powder box to harness the horse. The powder box came from the coal mines, which they had kept the explosives in. The coal miners would use the explosives to shoot the coal, so they could load it into the coal cars. I can remember my Grandparents saddling up a horse and sending me to the store. The store owner would open a hundred pound sack of feed and he would try pouring half of the feed in another bag, trying to equal them out. He would put the bag over the horses back, and sometimes I would have to take it off of the horse by my self. I would get on the other side of the horse and push it off. Then I would untie the bags so I could carry them in the barn. Fifty pounds was hard for me to carry into the barn at my age. When I was eight or ten years old, I would walk about four miles to take care of my aunt and uncle's garden and yard. I had to push the lawn mower, and that wasn't an easy job.

I remember one time and I don't know what age I was, my grandmother had some duck and geese. She and another lady on the ridge, would pick the feathers. They would make feather tick pillows out of the feathers. Now with all this said, the geese had some little ones in the pen. I was getting in the pen to play with them, but mama goose had a different plan. She attacked me and I went for the fence. She held me there and old papa goose gave me a whipping I still remember after seventy five years. Some times life was a little rough, but brother it might have been rough, but I ended up being Good Ole Country Boy.

I had an Aunt Vernie West. When Christmas came each year we were excited. She was only four years older than I was. We were more like brother and sister. We would go to the woods to get a Christmas tree. One Christmas there was about a foot or more of snow on the ground. Every tree that Vernie saw was the tree that she wanted. I would climb up the tree and cut the top out. Then she would decide that wasn't the one she liked, so we would go on to another tree. I would climb that tree and cut the top out, but that wasn't the right one either. This went on all day. I believe that I cut the top out of every tree in the woods.

I recall, when all the garden food was gathered in for the winter, there was only one thing left to get in and that was ground cherries, and brother was there plenty of them. Some of these cherries were purple and big. Others were yellow and small. We picked ground cherries up all day, and then we poured them on the front porch floor. The porch was about thirty feet long, and it was full of cherries. Vernie and I were getting tired, so we went back to the garden and laid down and rolled all over the rest of the cherries and smashed them. Then we went home and told Grandma we had gotten all of the ground cherries. I lived with Grandma and Grandpa until I was twenty years of age.

Another time I remember two of my uncles took me fishing. It was a beautiful Saturday after-noon. While fishing my uncle George, he got drunk and he was the driver. He had an old Plymouth truck. He always called me Gus. As we were coming back, every car we would meet he would say, Gus, you see that car coming, I'm going to hit it right between the eyes. He would stay over on the other mans lane and just before he got to him he would cut back over. He did this all the way back home. When got to the place to turn off he kept going on route ten going into Matoaka West Virginia. At the top of Matoaka mountain was a steep bank and brother I mean steep. My uncle George went to the top of the thing and it was pitch dark. It seemed as though we would turn over. He backed the thing off of there and we went home. I guess he got his kicks for the night. Now at that point and time I didn't fell like a good ole country boy. I would have felt much better at home bedded down in one of them feathered ticks.

Now some people might think it is crazy writing about people who have left this world many years ago and some of the things they said or told others. I think that it is wonderful. You know that I, a good ole country boy would like to be remembered for things that I have said. I hope and pray

that I have said something or done
something that has lightened some ones
load or lifted some ones hearts burden.
I have tried my best to encourage
people. You know it is better to laugh
than it is to frown. Now we will get
back to some of the things that could
be comical. My grand paw told me one
time when he was a young boy that
some one was stealing their neighbors'
corn out of their corn crib. There was
an air space between the strips so the
corn would dry good. This man would
put his hand between the strips, so my
Grandpaw put chicken wire and left a
place to put his hand. Then he set a
bear trap so he couldn't get his hand
out. The next morning he was standing
there by the corn crib just like a poor
ole, maybe I should just say raccoon.

I remember one time I had an
uncle that had a mule. That thing got
out and went to one of the neighbor's
house and went in and tore up a lot of
things in the house. The old mule
looked in the mirror, turned around,
kicked the mirror and tore the dresser
all to pieces. The lady put the old mule
in the barn and wouldn't let my uncle
have the mule back. She took him to
court, before the justice of the peace,
that's what they called them back in
the old days, (as we call them). So they
had their day in court and my uncle
came out on top. He got his mule back

and the justice of the peace told her he didn't want her back in his court. He didn't believe anything she said.

I had a great uncle who raised rabbits for a living. He had some retail grocery stores he sold his rabbits to. He would kill the rabbits then jerk their hides off and he would deliver them once a week. He really had the rabbits. I never saw so many rabbits. He had a wagon with shaves on it. He used a mule to get out to the main road. Then someone would take him and his rabbits to town and he would deliver them to each store. Well any way Uncle George didn't have a seat on his wagon, then he put the shaves on the fence and he went to work on the seat. He put springs on each end so it would give a better or maybe give him a smoother ride. He got it all put together. He calls for Aunt Mary to come over and they would try the seat out. They both sat on the seat. They got to bouncing up and down, and the wagon took off rolling down the mountain, but they didn't get hurt. All of this I've been writing about, all these things I've seen and heard makes me a Good Ole Country Boy.

I also had a great uncle that had a radiator shop in Bluefield West Virginia; there was a funeral home beside his shop. The funeral home had ordered some caskets and they didn't have enough space for all that he had ordered. They asked my uncle if he could store them upstairs at his place. He said yes, but if you don't mind leave one down stairs. Uncle Neely went home and told his wife that he had bought his casket. He then told her he was going to take a bath and put his suit on with a white shirt and tie. They would then go down to the shop, he would get into the casket he had bought and she could tell him how he looked. By now, you're thinking my family were some kind of odd balls, well you know what? You're right. We've all been that and done that, but you know that is what it takes to be a good ole country boy. There was another time he had bought a blank pistol. He got a bottle of ketchup, and went into the bathroom and fired the pistol. When his wife went to check on him, there he laid with that ketchup mess all over him. She just about had a heart attack.

I would go to my dad's on Sundays. I had a step brother and he would want to play cowboys and Indians. I am sure you have all done this. In your little towns it was probably a lot of running from light pole to light pole, but here we ran from tree to tree, and pretended to shoot each other with play guns. I bet that now you can see I am one of those hillbillies.

There was a man that came to my dad's house. Dad had known him for years, and he had become a preacher. There was not one church in our community and he was looking for a place to hold a revival. Reverend Tilley asked about the little building across the road and dad told him that was an old cow shed. Reverend Tilley asked if they could take a look at it. They went to the little building across the road and Reverend Tilley said it would be fine. They could put saw dust on the floor, an isle down the center, and benches on each side of the isle. They made a little alter to sit up front. The altar was about four foot long. The preacher said, there will be souls saved at this little alter; and there were a lot of people saved there. The preacher said that my dad said under his breath, that he knew one that would be saved at that altar. From that little cow shed was born two little churches; and they still have services at both these churches. When they were ready to build these churches, the people bought two or three houses from the coal company that people had moved out of. As we were tearing them down, Kirby Lyle and I would go with dad as he went to work. This was in the winter months, and brother it was cold, and we didn't even have a fire to eat our lunch by. Dad had a ton truck; He would get off work, we would load up the lumber that we had torn down, and haul it to the places where the church was to be built. We would unload the lumber after dark. Now this wasn't very pleasant for this old boy, but I wouldn't take anything for the good ole times. Living thru those days would make you stand on your own two feet, but it was good for all of us. We have seen a lot of people that went to both of these churches and how they would go there and rejoice in the Lord. At last they have a place to go and rest their bodies and feed their soul from the man on high.

My dad was saved at that little cow shed and was called to preach. He preached about fifty years. In the beginning of his ministry he would come home from work, and ask Hettie if she could find something in the bible. She would find it and that is what he would preach about on Sunday. I don't think dad could read.

Once there came an insurance salesman by, and he said he was a preacher. I in turn told him that my dad was a preacher. He wanted to know where my dad went to school to preach. I told him that he didn't go to school. The salesman replied that if he didn't go to school, that he couldn't preach. I told my dad what he had said, and dad clapped his hands together. It sounded like a rifle going off. He said; Bless God; put the two of us in the pulpit, turn the lights off and see who is preaching when the lights come back on.

I remember a man by the name of Coy Kinzer. He had come to my dad's house. It was in the winter months and it was blue cold (if you know what that is). Coy was one of those men who didn't have a home or family. When he visited my dad's house, they would let him sleep in the back room. Dad had oil stove in that room. They didn't hear a peep out of him all night, so before dad went to work, he went to check on Coy. Coy's head was as black as a pot. The oil stove had blown up and the black soot was all over Coy's head. Dad said; oh my God, I've killed Coy Kinzer. Coy got out of the bed and cleaned himself up. He then looked like a new man.

Coy would also come to my Grandpa's house. There was a building that Coy would pull his Nineteen Twenty Eight Ford up to and park. He would get out and put blocks against the wheels so the car wouldn't roll off. He would then drain the water out of the radiator, then come into the house and speak to everyone. He would sit down in front of the fire and roast his feet. I remember one time that my

Uncle George West would get him fussing until he would want to fight. Once Coy was playing his banjo and Garland Dunford told Coy that he was going to take a chair and make a picture frame over his head. Coy replied: and I will take this banjo and make you a neck tie if you mess with me. Now seeing all of this as a young lad, makes me feel like a Good Ole Country Boy. It seems that I dwell on the old timers, but I loved those ole timers. I wish I knew more about them. Once, my dad told me a tale about Coy. They had someone to write a letter to President Roosevelt. I can't recall who it was that wrote the letter, but I think Mr. Burton knew something about it. I think Mr. Burton was the one who wrote the response to the letter. Dad said they had taken the letter to the mines, had someone with a typewriter to fix up an official looking envelope and put some kind of a Washington postmark on the envelope. Dad told me that when Mr. Burton handed Coy the letter that he couldn't look at him without laughing. Coy took the letter and showed everyone in the store. Coy couldn't read or write, so he had some lady in the store to read it to him. The letter read something like this; if Coy Kinzer causes the tax payers any more trouble, and they write the president of the United States again; That the government would come pick him up and prosecute him to the fullest extent of the law. Now this didn't go over very well with Coy. He wasn't satisfied with what the lady read in the letter, so he went from house to house to have other people to read him the letter, and everyone was reading the same thing over and over. All of these people have gone on to get their rewards, and here I am writing about things they have done over Seventy Five years ago. Now tell me if it wasn't good being raised in Beeson, West Virginia.

There was another time that Coy was riding his bicycle. Someone jumped out of the brush in front of him and said give me your money; Coy replied I only have two dollars and you ain't getting it. Coy picked up his bicycle and ran.

My Grandpa and Grandma West had told me about the old crank phones. This was before my time. They said that Uncle Jimmy Foley would take the receiver off of his phone about five o'clock in the morning. Then the others would take their receivers off and Uncle Jimmy would stand in front of his phone and begin to play his fiddle. They told me he would play for about an hour, and that they all looked forward to that every morning. Now won't that just fire up your wood. There is so much history about these old timers, and I have enjoyed writing about them. While growing up in Beeson, West Virginia, I wish I had known more about them. While I was around them, I kept one ear cocked to see what they were going to say next. I believe I am a better person by just being around them at an early age in my life. I believe this is one of the reasons I can call myself a Good Ole Country Boy, and I am going to claim that title.

I was told of these two men at an early age. They would go to church once a month. That's the only time they would have church. They were of the Hard-shell Baptist Faith; that is what they called them. Here in Beeson, we called them Primitive Baptist Faith. I don't know why they got the name of Hard-shell. I was told by different people that Uncle Jimmy Foley, his wife, and Ballard Mills and his wife went to church together. After church Jimmy had asked the Mills couple to come to their house for dinner. They didn't have a car to ride to church, so they had to walk about four miles to the church. I wonder how many people now days would walk four miles to worship the Lord. I would say they are few and far between. Uncle Jimmy lived on top of a mountain and some Walker Families lived down in the valley. They were democrats and Uncle Jimmy was

republican. There came a frost one
night. Uncle Jimmy told someone; just
look down there in the Valley. The
frost, eat all those democrats up and
just look, the frost stopped at my fence
line.

When I was young, there was a
family by the name of Mills. They
called the old man Liquor Charlie and I
believe he lived up to his reputation.
The ones I knew were good to my wife
and I, but they butchered a few people.
I remember taking groceries to Mr.
Lilly's. I think that was his name. Jack
Mills stayed with the Lilly's a lot, and
this time, Zack was there. He had been
drinking and he asked me to take him
to Princeton to get some liquor. I told
him that I didn't have time, and he said
if you don't take me, I pity you. So I
took him. He was telling me about a
man he had killed, and the police had
him in the back seat of the police car.
They were going to jail, and the
policeman asked him how many men he
had killed. Zack said, I don't know
right off hand how many. The police
said maybe we better pull over and
search him again, and they did. I was
being kind to him at that time, but at
that time, I wasn't sure I was a Good
Ole Country Boy or not. The people in
our area said that Liquor Charlie had
killed some people back in the
mountains. He really had a good place

to make liquor, and I think he sold it to make his money. Some said that a traveling salesman went into the mountains, and never came out. Some said that liquor Charlie made the man eat a large cabbage head and it killed the man. There wasn't many people that would go back in those mountains. The part that I recall the most is when Liquor Charlie came to my Grand-fathers house selling black-berries. He was riding a horse, and when he got off of the horse he was all bent over, and walking with two canes. My dad and I went to their house when Liquor Charlie was on his death bed. He would crook his left arm and say the poor little thing wanted to live. They told that early in his life he had put a needle in the soft spot of a babies head. There was another man that rode his horse to their house. He got off the horse and tied it to a corner post. Mr. Mills said that the devil was out on the porch, do something with that devil. The gentleman went out, got onto his horse and rode off. He went home, got into his truck and left until Liquor Charlie was dead and buried. All of this was a mess.

I remember when I was about sixteen years old; my dad bought a team of horses and a farm. I had to plow the field. It took me five or six days to plow this large field. I would also plow some of our neighbor's gardens. Once, I was plowing and the point of the plow hit something. I don't remember what broke on the ploy, but I had the check lines around my neck and under my arm. The horses took off and drug me across the plow and that wasn't a pleasant ride.

One time, I wanted to go to the movies. We would have to walk six miles to Matoaka to see a movie. I asked my Grandmother for a quarter. She said she didn't have a quarter. Well, I knew better, because she handled all the money in that house hold. My Grandfather and I were riding up the hollow, and I asked him for a quarter. He gave me one and said; don't you tell your Grand-mammy I gave you that quarter. My lips were sealed. It was Saturday, and I was off to the movies.

When I was about sixteen or so, one Saturday, I had walked to the store and post office. While I was there I bought an oatmeal cake. I ate the cake on my walk home. By the time I got home I was sick. I was sick all of Saturday night and Sunday. On Sunday they took me to a doctor in Matoaka; he said I just had an upset stomach. On Monday morning, I was still sick, but I wasn't hurting quite as bad as I had been. They took me to another doctor in Matoaka and he told my Grandmother to get me to a hospital as soon as possible. One of my uncles had taken us to Matoaka in his old Model T Ford; I think it was a nineteen twenty eight model. He was having problems with the car and he had the hood up. The doctor came to the door and yelled, get that boy to the hospital or I am going to call an ambulance. My uncle dropped the hood and off we went to the hospital. When we arrived at the hospital the doctor said we have to get to the operating room now. When they took me into the operating room I could see saw's, and axes hanging on the wall. That didn't appeal to me at all. The doctor walked in and said we have got to get your appendix out because they have ruptured. He gave me a spinal shot. They had rolled me up like a knot to give me the shot. I wanted to straighten out, but I couldn't because the nurses were holding me down. As the doctor began surgery, the spinal shot had not done what it was supposed to. He began to split my belly. You could hear me yelling all over the town of Princeton, but not for long, because they then put the gas to me and I was out. I spent seventeen days in the hospital with a drain tube in my stomach. They had to change my bed twice a day due to the infection draining out. Now you can see that a Good Ole Country Boy had bad days also.

I recall that just before the Second-World War, there was something in the sky. It was like an ocean of blood. There was a huge roar along with it. Some people said it was the northern light. Now I don't believe that for one minute. My Great-Grandmother and Grandmother said our Lord would come that night. That had us all in an uproar. We were scared to death about going to bed. This thing went on about all night, and I will always believe this was from the higher power. I will always believe that the good man has a lot of things that he can show us. Let us not forget that he has the power.

My Grandparents raised a boy by the name of Willard Hawkins. His people had left him and his sister on a store porch over on the works. Later on, up in the years, my dad had bought him some long handled underwear. When he was ready for bed, he put the long handles on. He groaned all night. Dad went into Willard's room the next morning, and Willard told him, I just can't wear this underwear, its cutting my breath off. Dad looked at them and Willard had them on upside down. He had his head thru the trap drawer, in the back of the underwear. No doubt, the man was in pain.

When I was a child the young people would get together at some ones home. Some of the boys and girls would play post office. I don't remember exactly how the game was played. There would be one of the girls out there in the dark and one of the boys would go out there and kiss the lady that was in the dark. We really had a good time. There would be a wood fire or a lantern hanging there somewhere. In the fall of the year we would go to the molasses makings. Some of the young teenagers would go to sop the pan after they would get the molasses all jugged up. I will tell you right now, that raising cane is a tough job. My hat is off to those people who do it. During the summer months, we would go down to the creek and carry rocks to dam up the water. On some of the hot days, we would go there and lay in the creek. There I would lie in the water doing nothing but suffering pure comfort. Now, don't you wish that you would have been a good ole country boy? If you would happen to come from the city to these hills of West Virginia, and you were to go to the mountain and dark were to fall upon you, I'll tell you what to do. Just catch a opossum, tie a string around his tail and he will lead you back to the road.

In the early days, the teachers would let the community come to the school to have a pie supper. Mr. Shrewsbury would auction the pies off. He would say now gentlemen a pretty girl made this pie. What's your bid? This is a good pie. Now what are you going to give? I've got five now who bids six? The man who bought the pie had to eat the pie, with the lady who baked the pie. Brother, that school would be packed. The people that went there, and the teachers really enjoyed themselves. They and many others would spend a lot of money that night. They would also have cake walks. The couples would form a circle or a line, which ever you would like it to be. Soon after the auction couples would start forming circles. There would be so many couples that they would have to walk along the school walls. Mr. Shrewsbury would get the stick. It would be four or five feet long. He would then watch the clock. When it would come to the time he had set, he would drop the stick in front of some couple and they won the cake. I don't recall how much it cost, but I believe the proceeds went to the school for things they had going on. I do know for a fact that it was good for the community.

I remember the people around in the community talking about how they would go from house to house and dance. This was all the entertainment they had, and all of this was before my time. My dad would tell me all about these events. He told me about one weekend when Mr. Cecil had a big corn field that had to be hoed. The young men about wanted to have a dance at Mr. Cecil's home. The young people all gathered in to hoe the corn. Someone of the bunch asked Mr. Cecil how long they were going to dance, and Mr. Cecil replied; how long have you hoed corn? The young man said all day long, Mr. Cecil said; then we will dance all night long. This was good news for all these young men. This reminds me of a peace of scripture in the Bible where it tells about when men were hired. Some early of the morning and some were hired for later on in the afternoon. All got paid the same amount of money. I can almost see all of those city slickers there wishing they were a Good Ole Country Boy.

I recall a neighbor coming to our house one night wanting me to go coon hunting with him. He had bought himself a coon hound that was out of this world. I think he paid around five hundred dollars for this hound. Back in those days, five hundred dollars was equal to about five thousand dollars in the days we are living today. In those days, money was money, and now it doesn't mean anything. If we blow it, there will another check in the mail in the next couple of days. Now, back to the coon hound. We had walked up on a ridge in the woods and the hound had treed a coon on another ridge. We walked down the mountain, and up the other side. When we got there, shone the light up in the tree, there wasn't a coon to be seen anywhere and the old dog laid at the root of the tree. We got to moving around a little and the dog left us again. This old dog had a deep bass bark, sort of like me trying to sing bass. Anyway, the dog let out a bark down in the hollow. The man I was with said, now he is on to something. Then the dog went to another ridge and let out a deep bass bark. We walked all the way over there, and there is not a coon to be seen; that dog walked us to death and it was a while before I would go coon hunting again. The reason I remember this so well was because it was the day before my grand-father (the man that raised my sister and I), died in February of Nineteen Hundred and Forty Nine.

I had an uncle that I would go to visit on weekends; occasionally. His name was Guy. He had fox hound. About every Friday night he and some of his hunting friends would go fox hunting. Sometimes on Saturdays I would go with Uncle Guy to look for his dogs. He would let me sit on his lap and steer the truck. I wasn't very old and at this young age I thought I had really done something big. Uncle Guy had a milk cow that he wanted to sale. He put a sign up at the road in front of his house. A fellow by the name of Hobert came to see the cow. He asked Uncle Guy if this was a good milk cow? Uncle Guy told him that she had been a good milker. Guy told him that his Granddad had raised his family with milk from her, and his father had raised his family with milk from her, and I have raised my family with milk from her and I can say she has been a good milker.

BURTON STORE

As a young boy, I can only remember one grocery store. They had anything that you might need, including clothing, food, animal feed, and hardware. If you needed something they didn't have the owner would say I will have a car load in tomorrow. They had salt fish in a wooden barrel. Some of the sales men would spend the night with the store owner; who was also the post master. His name was O.H. Burton. He was the finest man I ever saw in my life. I would go to the store three or four times a day. Mr. Burton trusted me more than he did the others. After his wife passed away, he had taken a liking to the bottle or as some here in West Virginia call it laurel and pine stomp. As I said he was a fine man, but you didn't want to cross his path, or you were in trouble. Mr. Burton and his wife kept people in their home. Most of them were kindred. One was Uncle Green Richmond. He was a preacher. He would sit in the store around a pot bellied stove in the winter time, with his eyes closed. He sure could tell some wild tales. I do not believe what I am about to tell you, but here it goes. On Saturday evening he would ride his horse to a place called Barkers Ridge. There he would spend the night, and preach on Sunday. On his way there, going thru a place we all call Boggs Flats, he came upon some men that were drinking moonshine. They asked him if he wanted a drink. He told them no that he was a preacher. He said the men then held him down and poured the moonshine down him. Then on his way back home, he came upon the same men again. They asked if he would like a drink of moonshine, he said no, but you could drench me if you want to. Once he was telling a story about making moonshine. He told that one day the police came along, and something had happened to their moonshine steel, it was running across a country road. Now no doubt they were not at the moonshine still. If they had been, they would have had a bad day.

Mr. Burton and guests

When speaking with Stan from Bailey Kirk Funeral Home. He reminded me that there was another man who was a store owner in Beeson years ago. After Stan brought this to my attention, my brain kicked in. The store owners name was Mr. Maxwell. He was also a postmaster. As I recall, Mr. Maxwell has a crippled body. He waited on his customers. My father in law would buy a lot of things from him. Mr. Maxwell did a lot of business. He served his community well. I would like to thank Stan for bringing this history to my attention.

There was another older gentleman in the community of Beeson, by the name of Mr. John. I have been to their home many, many times. I would stay there until after dark just to listen to his tales. I will tell of one of his tales about my wife and I, before we were married. My wife's parents lived out in the country. There was a gate going off the country road to their house. There was sand all around the gate. Mr. John told that my girlfriend had gone to church, some ole boy walked her home that night and I had gotten word of this. Someone said they had seen me the next day. I was down on my hands and knees, then I rose up and said; Hee, Hee he didn't take her home, he just followed her home. When Mr. John was a young lad he would follow the threshing machine around. They would go from farm to farm to thrash wheat or buck wheat. Mr. John told that he would carry water for the men and sometimes he would tie the bags after they had been filled. They used to call him the young gentleman of the bunch. One day they asked the young gentleman if he would like to have some ground hog. He said yes-um I would, to one of the women, who was minding the table. Another woman was shewing flies off the vittles with a towel. As the young gentleman put a fork in the ground hog, and began to carve the meat with a knife, the ground hog kicked off the table, and onto the floor. Just then a little dog grabbed the meat and ran. Then a little white headed boy took off after the dog. He was gone for a bit, and upon his return he said; Mam, old Puck didn't get away with this ground hog. She said; son, be real nice and give the young gentleman back his groundhog. Now that was a good tale.

Mr. John would raise a small garden. He would take his vegetables to the coal fields. There were times when he would take eggs and sometimes he would also take chickens. One day a lady asked him to catch her a nice ground hog. Later he went out and caught a groundhog. He kept it until he went back to the coal field later in the week. He took the ground hog to the lady. She looked at it and asked Mr. John; are you sure this ground hog ain't with some, which means is she carrying little ground hogs. Since she wasn't carrying little one she decided to keep the ground hog.

Mr. John had to travel from Beeson across a mountain. There was a little white headed boy that would throw rocks at Mr. John when he came back from peddling. One evening, Mr. John caught the little white headed boy, and put him on the wagon with him. The little boy said; Mr. John please let me go and I'll never throw another rock at you. Mr. John took the little boy on down the road a ways. It was starting to get dark, and the little boy said Mr. John, if you will let me go, I will never throw another rock at you. Mr. Tom let the little boy go, and as soon as he did, the little boy threw a rock at him. Mr. John got off of his wagon and the little boy left out and headed home. That little white headed boy grew up and I was then a young lad. Mr. John would be coming home from work and would say to me; I was trying to take his girl friend, but you know I was a little bit young for that. He would then tell me that if I didn't quit trying to take his girl friend that he was going to cut my ears off. I began to believe him, when I would see him coming, I would hide.

After taking his girlfriend for his wife; I bet he would have loved it if I had been old enough to take her. Now this is one of those things that bring out the life of a Good Ole Country Boy.

Mr. John had a door in front of the house and straight back from the door was a window. He would lean his chair back against the window, so he could see all the movements going up and down the road. Brother he didn't miss anything going on. There were two holes in the floor that the back legs of his chair sat in. I'd say the holes were about an inch deep. I wish these days now were like those days. Automobiles and television has taken all of our time. You see we can't even read our bibles these days, because of our favorite television shows. People, I'm in the same boat with you. I have as much guilt as others.

Mr. John told of another tale as follows: he said there were two boys who were stealing from a merchant but he couldn't catch them in the act. One Sunday he saw them stealing cookies, when he went after them, they ran. They ran down a long ridge behind the store. They got about half way down the ridge, and then they stopped and turned. They saw that the merchant was still coming, so one of them put the cookies in the bosom of his shirt. As they came to the end of the ridge, there was a pond of water. At the pond there was something in the pond, black, and dressed in white. The boys turned, and there was the merchant behind them, so the boys then jumped in the pond. The black people of the community were having a baptism. The preacher reached over and nabbed one of the boys, the one with the cookies in his bosom. The preacher dunked the boy under the water, brought him up and asked, brother do you believe? The boy said nothing, the preacher dunked him again and asked; son, do you believe? The boy said nothing. About that time the cookies were starting to crumble and float to the top of the water. A sister in the back started looking thru the crowd of people and said sock him under again his sins are coming out in chunks. The preacher dunked him again. When he brought the boy back up, the preacher asked; son, do you believe? The boy then replied I believe you are trying to drown me. Ah, Mr. John was one of a kind. He was one in a million.

Mr. John's wife was preparing a meal to take to church on Sunday. They only had church once a month. On that day, they all took a dish. After church services, they would all sit down and have dinner and conversations. They really enjoyed their day. On Saturday, Mrs. John had baked five apple pies, and placed them in the cabinet. There had been a homeless man, (Garland), who went from house to house, because he had no family, and he stayed at Mr. John's home while they were out to church. Mrs. John had taken one of the pies she had baked to church and left the other four at home. When they came back home they couldn't find the pies or Garland. After a while they heard him behind the old wood burning cook stove, carrying on something awful. Mr. John looked at him and then he looked at the cabinet. He then said, "Yat gad durn ya" you ought to die; you ate all of Callie's (Mrs. John) pies. Once one of the people in the community had gone to Mr. John's house, and he and Callie were eating dinner. Mr. John asked this man if he would like something to eat. The man refused. Mr. John said "Yat gad durn ya" don't you go off and tell that Callie wouldn't give you anything to eat.

Another story that the old timers told me was; as you know, in the early days, when a person would die, the lady folks would get the body ready for burial and the men would make the casket. A lady in the community had died. They had her laid out for a week. When the lady folk got the body ready, the man of the house went in to view the body. Everything looked OK to him so he called out for the youngin's. Get in here and look at your Mammie, she has done chased her last cat. Now if that don't make your ding dong ding, I don't know what would. For me, I wouldn't begin to utter those words, because I have told you, I am a good ole country boy.

Once my uncle had bought himself a high powered model T Ford, with the gear shift in the floor. He loved that power house of a car. One day he and another one of my uncles were going some-where, and the car stopped in the middle of the road. Both men had on bibbed overalls. The man that owned the high powered car had the hood up. The other one got out, and was standing there with his hands down inside his bibbed overalls. He asked him what the problem was. My uncle said, the motor is missing. The other uncle replied; I thought it was in there when we left. I bet you are saying to yourself, that I would have much rather been a Good Ole Country Boy instead of a city slicker.

I was blessed to live in the Nineteen Thirties and up until now in the Two Thousands. There were a lot of old timers that I knew. All of them liked me and I liked all of them. I can give you an example of one of our old timers that liked me. I'll call him Uncle Allen. He and I would go to the cattle market together. I would take him to pick up the feed for his cattle, hogs, chickens, and horses. I would also take him to the doctor, he had prostate cancer. His son worked in the coal mines and was a preacher. The day after I took Uncle Allen to the doctor, his son stopped by and asked what the doctor said. I told him what the doctor had said. He looked at me with a half way grin and said he didn't believe that, but after a little while, he came to grips with it. The last time I saw Uncle Allen, he was on his death bed, I started to leave, so I shook hands with him and he said; Lawrence, I have a lot of confidence in you, and I hope that you have a lot of confidence in me also. I had a great friend, and that's why it's so good to be a good ole country boy. If all men were like this man, in the days we live in now, what a great country we would have. Now, you can see some of the things that I was blessed with, I was brought up in a wonderful time, knowing these people.

I was told that Mr. Bill had gone and asked Mr. John when would be best time was to kill hogs, according to the signs in the moon, so that there wasn't so much fat. Mr. John told him the right sign to kill in. Mr. Bill killed the hogs at the time that Mr. John had told him to do so. Mr. John came along, and Mr. Bill told him that he had killed the hog when he said to, and the meat was nothing but fat. Mr. John replies: Yat gad durn ya, you killed it wrong, you killed it a moon too soon. They fell out over it. Mr. Bill said: I god sir, you can't travel across my property anymore, and that's that. Mr. John had to build a road above Mr. Bill's property. I give you the tales I was told. They might be right or they might be wrong, but after seeing and or hearing these things, that's what makes me a Good Ole Country Boy.

Mr. Bill lived up in the hollow a ways from O.H. (Mr. Burton) the store keeper. One evening Mr. Burton and I were sitting on the porch of the store, and Mr. Bill came walking down by the store. Mr. Burton Asked Mr. Willie (Mr. Bill) as some called him, what do you know? Mr. Bill replied: Mr. Burton, if I told you what I know, then you would know what I know and what you know too. Another time Mr. Bill was walking by the store with tools on his back. Mr. Burton asked him: what have you been doing Willie? Willie said I have been pruning apple trees for Bill Harmon. Mr. Burton said Willie you can't do that, you don't have a pruner's license. Willie replied; I-got-sir I can prune as good as a man with a pruners license, and down the road he went. Once Mr. Bill came into the store late in the evening, and there were no lights. He had bought some items and was due fifty cents back in change; Mr. Bill dropped the change on the floor, and couldn't find it. Another boy and I were in the store. With tears in Mr. Bills eyes, he said I-got-sir one of those boys got my money. The next day, Mr. Burton found the fifty cents behind the post office wall. That was good news for me and the other boy that was in the store, or he would have gone thru life thinking that we had his money.

Mr. Burton had a dog and his name was Rover. One morning Mr. Shrewsbury came by with his dogs, and his dogs really tore Rover up. That really set Mr. Burton off. That evening Mr. Burton saw Mr. Shrewsbury coming with his dogs, and Mr. Burton met him at the end of the steps with his gun. Mr. Burton was really mad. He even had tears running down his face. Mr. Shrewsbury was standing with one foot up on the stairs and the other on the ground. He stood that way for some time. One of the dogs was looking thru Mr. Shrewsbury's legs. Mr. Burton said if you say one damn word, I will shoot that damn dog between your legs.

Mr. Burton would close up shop at seven o'clock and go to the house to listen to Edward R. Murl on the radio. We didn't have televisions to watch and there was no electricity for light. They had to burn a carbide tank. I don't know how many kegs of carbide they would pour in a tank. I don't know how long it would take to use a tank of carbide. They had the store and the house running on the same tank. They had little pipes that ran to both the house and the store. These little pipes had little heads on the ends that you light.

I'm now going to tell you about a man who never went to church anywhere, because it was quite a distance to walk. This man was a hard working man and one of the most humble men I have ever been around. He would sit around at night time and read the Bible, with a cat and a dog on his lap. He chewed tobacco and I guess that's why I picked up the habit. It must not be all that bad, because I'm seventy five years old and I still chew.

There was a city slicker that came to the country once. He fell in love with one of these West Virginia gals. After he saw one of these country girls, there became a yearning in his heart for one of these gals. Later he married one of those West Virginia gals. The first weekend after their marriage, he wanted to help his new mother-in-law while she made breakfast. His mother-in-law gave him a milk bucket and a stool and sent him to the barn to milk the cow. He went out of the house whistling. Breakfast was ready,

everyone else had eaten. After all this
time, he still hadn't come back, so the
mother-in-law went to look for him. He
was still in the barn with his pretty
white shirt on, and it was a mess. He
looked at his mother-in-law and said; I
can't get that cow to sit on the stool so
I can milk her. Now you see it is better
to be a good ole country boy, we know
that we have to sit on the stool to milk.

I wasn't around when this happened. But some of the family
enlightened me, about a man that came
to their home and darkness had fallen
upon him, so he stayed all night. They
had given him a bed, upstairs. After a
while he went upstairs to go to bed.
During the night, one of the brothers of
the family had gotten under his bed. He
came up on his hands and knees and
rolled the man out of the bed. The man
got up and headed for the stairs. One of
the other brothers was at the bottom of
the stairs, wearing a white sheet with
his arms stretched out, and waving his
arms. The man thought it was an angel,
so he went back to bed. He lay there
awhile, and then he was rolled out of
the bed again. He wouldn't go down the
stairs because an angel was at the
bottom of the stairs waving, and a devil
was under his bed. It was my
understanding that this went on all
night. At the break of dawn, the man
left there and said; dark would never

catch him there again. I would say that poor man did have a rough night. If I had been this man; I wouldn't have been back there in the daylight either.

My grandfather died in the year of our Lord, 1947. I was seventeen at that time. I've told many people that if Grandpaw West didn't make it to heaven, there was no use of us trying. These two people that raised my sisters and I were wonderful people. I left Grandmaw at the age of twenty. She had a son by the name of Ralph. Ralph lived in Virginia. He came to visit one Saturday evening. He met me on the walk and said that I had laid around for his mom to take care of. He told me that I was a lazy good for nothing. It was then that I packed my stuff and left, not knowing that he had brought his son. The law had told Ralph that he had to get his son out of the state of Virginia or else. Now you see Grandmaw traded a good ole country boy for one of the bad boys in Virginia.

Later on I will talk about those good ole West Virginia Girls. Oh my how sweet they are. I will tell you right now, those honey bees we talked about earlier, don't have anything on these country girls. I married one of these girls, and she was the apple of my eye. The first time she saw me, she laughed out loud. She still took me under her wing and she was sweeter than the honey those bees made.

There is another old gentleman I would like to tell you about. His name was Cal Blevins. He had a large family. I never knew of him working in public works. He may have early in his life, but I don't recall it. He was real old at the time I knew him, but what fascinated me was how he would take care of his bees. He had a lot of bees, and he kept a chair in the middle of all the bee hives. He didn't wear any protection to keep the bees from stinging him. He sat there everyday seven days a week, weather permitting. Cal had a lot of beard on his face. When the weather was warm and I am talking about eighty to ninety degrees, at this time of the day, the bees would swarm. Each hive had a queen bee, and if you could get the queen bee back into the hive, then knock on the hive, the rest of the bees would go into their hive. You see, this is why I like to call myself a Good Ole Country Boy; you can't sit on third or fourth street and get in on all this action, so I say God Bless these wonderful mountains of West Virginia. If you haven't been to see these mountains come on by, you may like what you see, you may want to bring your bunk bed and stay a while.

There was a man by the name of Gilmer Harvey that lived in our community. He was loved by everyone.

His mind wasn't right. He was very happy with everyone that he was around. And everyone enjoyed being around him. People picked at Gilmer all the time. He would go to church every time the doors were open. He would go to the alter to pray and whoever he had on his mind, was who he prayed for. He would pray over and over again. I would have liked for him to pray for me. His entire heart, soul and mind was in his prayers, because he loved everyone that he prayed for. People would pull pranks on him all the time, and he would get tickled. I remember once a long time before Faye and I married; Ray was driving the pick-up truck and we stopped at a beer joint. We didn't go in, but the man who owned the beer joint was sitting outside. We got Gilmer off of the truck, and he started preaching. Faye, Ray and myself got back into the truck like we were going to leave, but Gilmer just kept on preaching. Ray would pull the truck up a little and then stop. Then Gilmer would start preaching; this went on for well over an hour.

The church was just past our house. Faye, Joanna (our oldest child) and I would be in the bed, Gilmer would come thru the yard and yell, Hey Jo. Then he would clear his throat and yell Hey Jo. He really liked little Joanna. Once I had a little pig. He had gotten out of his pen, and I had him hemmed up in the barn. Here came Gilmer talking and laughing saying get him brother Lawrence and that's when the pig left there.

Faye Peyton West

Douglas and Annie Peyton
(Faye's Parents)

I would like to tell you a little about my wife. She was born here in Beeson, West Virginia. She and I had started dating when she was thirteen years old. We lived about four miles of each other. Around that time there was maybe five or six houses between us. Now you can see how many times people got around in the neighborhood. Isn't that amazing? Faye's parents had a farm house on Nubbins Ridge. Faye and I were planning on getting married. Faye, her mother and I had gone somewhere one night, and we were talking to her mother about our plans. Annie (Faye's Mother) said that I needed to ask Douglas (Faye's Father) for permission. Annie said if I didn't ask him he might get angry. Now to be honest, that was something I wasn't looking forward to. I went to their house the next morning to pick Faye up. We were going to get the blood test for our upcoming marriage. While I was waiting for Faye to get ready, I asked Mr. Peyton if he had any objections to Faye and me getting married. He was sitting there reading the newspaper and it seemed like he read that paper for two days before he put it down. He pulled his glasses off and swiped his face then he said; I would just as soon you have her as anybody he knew of. Oh boy was that a relief. I married into one of the best families. I was blessed to be a part of that family. There are not many who can say that. They are all gone now. There is only two daughter-in-laws, and one son-in-law (myself) left. Faye's parents had a large house and we would all gather there on weekends. We had the best times there together. This was one of the best nitted families that you would ever see. They were full of jokes and pranks. They all loved the other, and it was a joyous time. Faye's father was full of himself. He would pull one on you, and never crack a smile. Faye and I hadn't been married but a couple of weeks and everyone was sitting at the table. Everyone was either eating or passing food. They had a big long table. Mr. Peyton passed me some hot pepper and said; you better get some of this, it will put lead in your pencil. I was sitting there, my face red. I believe if someone had struck a match, I would have blown up. Everybody sat there laughing and looking at me and Mr. Peyton just sat there eating as if everything was OK. My brother-in-law Ray and I were both in the Korean War at the same time. He was released two or three weeks before I was. After I came home, Faye, Ray and I went to pick some wild grapes. We were planning to make some grape wine. We made the wine and put it in the cellar. Later on in the winter time, we were sitting around playing cards and Ray happened to think of that wine. I don't remember who went and got it, but Ray tried to open it and he couldn't so he gave it a shake. Willow, (Faye's brother), said give it here, but he couldn't get the top off so he gave it a shake and handed it over to Chester (another brother of Faye's). He tried to turn it and he couldn't get the top off either. Mr. Peyton said give me that jar. Chester gave it a shake and handed it over to Mr. Peyton. You see they were setting things up for Mr. Peyton. Mr. Peyton turned that cap off of the jar and wine went everywhere, clear up to the ceiling. Mr. Peyton capped his mouth over the jar, his jaws began to bulge, and his face turned red. He was motioning for someone to get the jar, but no-one would get it, so he drank all he could hold. It was taking his breath, so he removed the jar from his mouth and wine hit the ceiling again. After all was said and done, Mr. Peyton said boys you all could have gotten that cap off. Now you can see what joy there is in being a good ole country boy. I wouldn't take anything for the experience I've had being a country boy, but all of my life wasn't roses. I have had my ups and downs also.

I remember one Sunday, I two of Faye's brothers, and two of their sons had gone ground hog hunting. We dug into a nest of young ground hogs. We didn't have anything to put them in, so I pulled my coverall off and tied the legs together. I don't know how many ground hogs there was, but I can tell you they were a load to carry out of those mountains. When we got home with them we showed everybody our catch. Then we turned them loose. I can remember a bunch of us going fishing one Saturday evening. We had gone down to New River. Two people had gone out on the boat, and set a trout line. After setting the trout lines, they came back to the river bank. It had been raining and the river was high and getting higher. One of Faye's brothers and I were going to check the lines. The other men shoved the boat out and we couldn't get the motor started. The water was pushing us down the river and there was some falls below. As we were getting closer to the falls, someone threw us a long rope. One of us caught the rope and the other men pulled us in. Now if the Lord hadn't been with us we would have been goners. Now you know it's a blessing to have our blessed Savior with us in times like this.

There were three men that have been a blessing to me time and time again over the years. Lacy, Earl, and Vester Akers. They were my wife's double first cousins, and I came to love them as if they were my children. They

would eat with us on holidays, and it
didn't matter how cold it was, they
were always here. These three brothers
lived together and never married. I had
a lot of cattle back in the sixties, and
they would always help me put up the
hay, hoe corn, or what ever I needed
done. They were very helpful and
would work ten or twelve hours a day
and never accept more than three
dollars a day for the work they had
done. If someone in the community
died, they were the first ones at the
cemetery to dig the grave. They served
in the army in the Second World War.
One of them received a purple heart.
Lacy, Earl and Vester depended on my
wife to take them to their doctor's
visits at the veteran's hospital. There
were times that they would be gone all
day and often not return home until
after dark. In those days; if you had an
appointment at ten o'clock, you might
get to see the doctor at 4 o'clock or
maybe later. I go to the veterans now,
and it is different now. They are pretty
well on time with their appointments.
One night we were out singing in
Virginia and we got home late. Earl had
gotten sick. When we got home someone
called and told us that Vester had been
at our house until way up in the night.
Earl was almost at death's door, but
Vester would not go to any other
neighbor's houses to call an ambulance.

Vester waited until day break, then came back to our house and knocked on the door. Our Sunday was well spent. We were glad to be with them in their time of need. Later on Earl passed away. After a while Lacy passed on, then my wife and I brought Vester to live with us. He fit right in with our children. We took care of him the best that we could until he passed away. We prayed that God was pleased with the care we had given each of these good men. Now you can see why I want to write about some of these people, and should write about them. These men and other men and women should be written about. These people were history and our families have lived with them and we should keep their names alive. Someday we will all be gone, and we will then be history. I am sure some of you would like to be remembered after you are gone. These three men I have been writing about are men in our community that has left a legacy and I believe they deserve to be remembered.

U. S. NAVAL SHIP MARINE ADDER

This is the Naval Ship *Marine Adder* I
rode on.

Lawrence and Faye West

After leaving my grandmother; on March 15, 1952, Lennettice Faye Peyton and I were married. This was the best thing that ever happened to me. My wife (Faye) and her parents took me under their wings just as if I were one of their own. Faye and I stood together thru thick and thin. Our love was bound thru Jesus. He was with us every step of the way. After being married a short three months, big Sam said he had a job for me; and I had no choice in the matter. It was really heart breaking to have to leave this beautiful, wonderful woman.

I went to boot camp; then I got to came home for Christmas, before going to Korea. My wife was expecting our first child in three weeks. I had heard so much about the Red Cross and how they helped people. I made a trip to their office in Bluefield, West Virginia. I asked for a leave from the army until after our child was born. They asked me how I got into this world. I said I was born into this world and they replied; you go on to Korea and your child will be born just like you were. I then told them, if you and the Salvation Army were standing side by side on the street with a tin cup that I would put a nickel in the Salvation Army's cup and I would spit in the Red Cross cup.

I was reluctant to tell about any of the time I had spent in the army, but a lot of people say that I should since it was a part of this good ole country boy's life. The more I thought about it, I decided to discuss it because serving this great nation of ours, where we have the freedom to enjoy so much today. Looking at other countries that do not have the same freedom that we enjoy, I feel it was an honor to serve our country. The day before we were to depart, the CEO gave us a talk. He told us if the ship was about to sink, to get as far away from the ship as you can. We knew if it happened to sink, it would draw us under with the ship. I was on a ship named the *Marine Ader*. After shipping out; the next morning there was a storm. I didn't know; we would ride the waves up and down. When we went to breakfast, and got our tray; you'd better hold on to it or it would go yonder end, and you better be on alert or it would pass you up. You talk about being sick, we were all sick. I thought about the things the CEO had told us, about the ship sinking, I thought he must have known it was going to sink, and I couldn't swim a lick. They said there were eighteen hundred men on the ship. It was in January when we got close to Hawaii, it was very warm. It had taken eighteen days to get there from Japan. When we

got off at the dock, and boarded a
train, they brought me a telegram,
telling me that my wife and new baby
girl and was doing fine. Everything was
alright. Now you know that this took a
load off of this ole country boy's heart.
At least I could sleep better at night.
The next day they put us on another
ship and sent us to Korea. You could
smell Korea from a hundred miles
away. When we got to Pusonn we stayed
there. There were fox holes to get in, if
it came to that. During the night, the
sirens began to blow. That was
incursion, my first night in Korea.
There wasn't much sleep that night. I
got into one of the fox holes. In a little
while there came someone right on top
of me, then came another. We survived
all of that. There was a plane, the
solders there called that plane Bed
Check Charlie. Later on we found out
all about Bed Check Charlie. The next
morning they put us on a train to Seoul
Korea. Along the way we found out
about scares of war. Little children
would be standing there wanting
something to eat, or drink. They were
dirty as could be, probably with no
mother or father. That would soften an
old stony heart. When we got to Seoul,
we were all split up and sent in
different directions. I ended up in the
Seventy Third trucking company, two
thirty first battalion. Sometimes it was

rough, but I was with a mighty fine bunch of men. Before I get into many details; there were four of us from this area. We had been split up at Fort Knox, Kentucky. Out of the four of us, I am the only one still living. Again I can say God has blessed this Ole Country Boy, and I thank him for it everyday of my life. Without him, I would be nothing. My tour in Korea has helped me along life's way. I hadn't been anywhere out of West Virginia, and it helped me to stand on my own two feet. It was an experience for me. Since I was in the trucking company that allowed me to see a lot of Korea, Genson, and way up on the east coast. One night we were in a convoy, and we drove all night long. I believe that was the most beautiful place I saw in Korea. We had some men in there that didn't care about anything. There were two men that stand out in my mind, Lanney and Luke. Both men had been in the army for several years, but they only ranked Corporals, and they stood together. I remember having a bar and a make shift bar. They had stools around the bar. Lanney was sitting on a stool and Luke was standing by him. They were both pretty much two sheets in the wind. You could get a can of beer for a dime. A fellow by the name of Tyson told Luke that he would give him five dollars if he would knock Lanney off of the stool. Lanney leaned over to Luke and said knock me off of the stool and we will split the five dollars. Luke drawled back and knocked him off the stool and onto the floor. We all got a kick out of that, and our good friend Tyson had to pay up. There was another man who called himself Baldie. Baldie had no hair on the top of his head. He would come into the bar and rub his head saying; Baldie, would you like a beer today; then he would say I don't know yet. Yeah, I believe I will take a beer. He came in once and yelled out, when Baldie drinks we all drink. Some of the other men went to the bar to get their free drinks. Then Baldie said; when Baldie pays, everyone pays. That didn't go over too well with those soldiers who gathered at the bar to get a free drink. Just think that beer cost all of a dime. That was big money then, if you were only getting thirty some dollars a month like me. Most of mine was going back home to my wife and child.

Baldie and friends

Lawrence West

Lawrence West

Home Away From Home

I remember one time I went to
Yongdong Po to the px to get a carton
of Hershey candy bars and a carton of
camel cigarettes. I rode in the truck. I
drove and carried our M-one all of the
time. It was very hot that day. When I
came back to the truck, I sat my M-one,
my cigarettes and candy in the
passenger seat. There were five or six
Koreans there on my side, just talking
up a storm. As I started to back out, I
looked down on the passenger side of
the truck, and all of my candy and
cigarettes were gone. Well, that's the
life of a good ole country boy. While I
was there, our company got new trucks.
They were equipped with air horns and
the whole nine yards. Now I had a
friend by the name of Calvert. One day
he was going to the px at Yongdonga;
driving his truck. You may know by
watching television, how the people
that lived there would carry their stuff.
Some men had long poles they carried
on their shoulders, with a bucket on
each end, and the women would carry
their load on their head. The women
would take their clothes to the Han
River to wash them. They would beat
dirt out of their clothes on a rock. The
roads were dirty, and we would have to
drive right above the river. I am going
to tell you what happened to one lady
that had been to the river to wash her
clothes. When she headed for home, she

had a plate like item on her head. I believe this plate measured approximately three feet wide, with all her clothes on it. As Calvert drove by; he blowed his air horn, and that woman ran out from under those clothes. Now you talk about someone that was laid out to the dogs, she really laid us out. She had to gather up all her clothes and go back to the Han River. I would guess that she said; this has been a long wash day. We really got enjoyment out of that, but we should have been ashamed. I remember very well when a truce agreement was signed on July, Twenty Seventh. I remember that night so well. We all had to stand guard, because the Koreans were going to attack us. I am talking about the South Koreans. The very ones we were fighting for. All night with no sleep our company Seventy Third trucking helped exchange prisoners. We picked up our prisoners at Panmunjom and took them to Inchon, where we were taking them to get on a ship. They were a weak bunch of men. Taking back the North Korean Solders to Panmunjom they were in really good shape. One morning, the captain called me to his office, he handed me a paper. He asked if I knew anything about the papers, and asked me what he should do with them. I looked at the papers. Some of grand-ma's people had gotten together

some papers to try and get me out of
the army. The papers stated that I
needed to come home to take care of my
grand-ma. I told the captain to put
them in the trash, and that's just what
he did. I was blessed for my Savior
looked out after me and that is why I
am a Good Ole Country Boy. With all of
this, you can see how a Good Ole
Country Boy had to live. I must stop
writing about this, I may have said too
much already.

After I came home from the Korean
War, I asked for my old job back. The
job I had before I went to the army.
They refused to let me go back to work,
so I drew my twenty three dollars per
week unemployment for twenty three
weeks. I had a wife and baby girl to
support, so I had to find work. I looked
here in West Virginia, but I couldn't
find a job for love or money. My
brother-in-law Ray and I went to
Columbus Ohio trying to find work. We
went to one place in Ohio and asked for
an application. One of the men asked if
we were ninety day wonders and
wouldn't give us an application. Again
we came home empty handed; and from
there we went to Norfolk Virginia, but
we had no luck finding a job there
either. Later on, my wife Faye and I
went to Pennsylvania trying to find
work. We had our baby girl with us
also. She would stand up in the seat

next to me with her little hand on my shoulder. As we pulled up next to Washington D.C. on a busy Sunday evening around three O'clock; a car in front of us slammed on his brakes, and I had to do the same. Joanna was thrown forward, close to the windshield and as she came back by my side she said the son-of-a-bitch. Now that just knocked our socks off because we never dreamed she would say anything like that. After all she was only two years old at the time. We had chosen Pennsylvania because Faye had a sister living there. Things were bad there also, but we thought we might have better luck finding a job there. Every place we went, we heard the same thing: thing are rough. There was one place we hadn't gone to yet. When we got there, they said they were not hiring. I told the man I was from West Virginia and that I had been discharged from the army. I had collected all of my unemployment, and that I had a wife and daughter to support. They questioned me for a bit and the man said I will be back in a little while. When he came back he asked me to come back at one o'clock that afternoon. My wife, my wife's sister, little Joanna and I went back and met with them. They asked if I could do any carpenter work. I said I have never done it before, but I am willing to try;

so they gave me a job doing maintenance. Boy oh boy was I pleased. I would be making one dollar and a quarter an hour, and work only forty hours a week. This was a chain saw factory. One Monday morning I went into the shop and the other two carpenters hadn't come to work yet. I waited around for about thirty minutes then the owner of the plant came in and he asked me if I could build a pair of steps. I told him that I had never built a pair before. He said I know you are just the man that can build them. He said you get your lumber and get to it. I went to the lumber yard, and with all the two by ten boards there was, I think I marked every one of them. I finally came up with a pattern that looked like what I needed. I cut the stairs out and put them together. When the boss came up that evening, he said; that they looked really good. I knew this morning, that you were the man for the job. After that I was ready for anything. If you have never cut out a pair of steps, it's not an easy task. Doesn't that just tickle your innards? If you know what I mean.

We didn't have a house to live in so we stayed with Faye's sister. After I got paid for the first two weeks work, we got an apartment. The bad part was that we didn't have any furniture to put in the apartment. We went to a flea market and got a table, and two chairs I believe it cost us two dollars. We bought a couch that would pull out and make a bed. By now I guess you know two young people who were pinching their pennies. This was in the year of Nineteen Fifty Five. I look around and about at the other young couples that had nice homes and new cars in their driveways, and in some cases there would be two cars. My wife and I didn't have much, and we were just one payday away from being homeless. I think most people would be out in the cold if they had to miss one payday. It didn't bother us because we didn't have anything to lose anyway. Later on when we got another payday, we went to a yard sale and bought an electric stove for five dollars. Boy oh boy, we went home rejoicing, because we had something we could bake some cornbread in, and fry some eggs on. We got the stove into the house, and when I started to hook it up, I put my hand back in the oven, and that thing sent me for a loop. After I had gotten myself back together, I said; there goes my cornbread and fried eggs. Later on, we bought a gas stove. I just couldn't handle those yard sales. There was another place we used to go to along with many other people. It was called Barns. It was on the outskirts of Oxford, Pennsylvania. They had about anything that you wanted, if you liked used stuff.

We were really accepted in Pennsylvania. The people were wonderful. We could leave home, and when we came back there would be fresh food from a garden waiting on us. There was a music park there and every Sunday there would be someone from the Grand Ole Opry there. The gentleman that owned the park had a rocking chair. He would sit in it and rock through the entire event. I remember one Sunday afternoon one of the Opry stars brought some moonshine. He took it out of his pocket and was going to show everyone how strong it was. He took a drink of the white lightening. He spewed it out into a box sitting beside the rocking chair, it exploded and smoke went everywhere. That old man jumped out of his rocking chair and broke to run off the stage. After seeing all these things, life has been good. I remember one Sunday they had introduced one of the stars from the Grand-Ole-Opry. I can't remember which one it was. When they introduced this man he came onto the stage putting his clothes on. The audience had a good laugh and the show went on. Another time, there was a man that didn't have any arms. He put his guitar on the floor, or someone else put the guitar on the floor. Then he began to play. He corded with one foot and played with the other.

While we were living in Pennsylvania, we had come in to visit with Faye's family. When returning home. We took two of her brother's children back with us, to stay for two weeks. On Friday night, we were bringing the children back home. While going thru Charles Town, West Virgina, there was a down pour of rain. There was a long line of traffic. In this line of traffic, I was pulled over by the law. They asked for my driver's license and registration. They kept my cards and told me to follow them to the police station. They said I had run a stop sign, and the fine was twenty five dollars. I told them I didn't have any money. They said I would have to go upstairs. I then told them that I had my wife and four children with me. They replied that they would take care of them. I then knew these guys meant business. I pulled about eight hundred dollars out of my pocket. The money was all rolled up together. The police officers looked at each other, like some-thing was going to happen. I paid the fine and we were on the road again. The police officer followed us for miles.

I had another good job in Pennsylvania. I worked at it for about four years. My wife's mother had been in a car accident in Princeton, West Virginia, and my wife had to come home to care for her. I was left to batch. There were something's that I just couldn't handle, so I told the super-intendent that I was leaving the company and going back to Beeson where my roots were; because my wife would be gone for a long while. The superintendent told me that he didn't want me to go. They gave me a cut off slip for six months, so that would give me a while to think it over. They said that if I didn't come back; that at anytime I wanted a job at any of their plants; that I would have a job. All I had to do was to call the main office. On my cut off slip they put that I was an above average worker, and brother that just knocked my socks off.

I was working at the sawmill. One day the whole crew had to go to the woods. It was hot. It was in July or August, and the boss told us to watch and listen for rattlesnakes because there were plenty of them in these mountains. One of the men spoke up and said there ain't no rattlesnakes up here. He said I was raised on top of these mountains. Low and behold he walked about a hundred foot into the woods and he walked up on a rattlesnake. Boy oh boy he was the grandpa of them all. They were talking about how they were going to catch him. There was a man there and he had a pair of high top boots. He took the boot laces and tied them together and then he got two forked sticks. One put a stick about six inches behind his head and one put a forked stick back next to his tail. There was a man they called Acie there. He made a loop with the shoe string and dropped it right over the snakes head. They led him right up the road and put him in the bed of a pick-up truck. Now at noon we went up to eat lunch and that fellow was doing some singing. That snake was about four and a half or maybe five foot long, and as well as I can remember it had eighteen rattlers and a button. We had a lot of fun on that job, and everyone was jolly and everyone worked together. Well it was a joy to work with men like that. There was an older like man (Lewis) that worked there and he stayed there all the time. They had him a building there to live in. He would cut his own hair. He would let it grow until he really needed one. Well some evenings after work he would cut one side then later on he would cut the other side. I remember one time we were eating our lunch and Lewis came in. Oscar asked him if he had a good dinner? Lewis said, I had a good can of pet milk.

One day three of us were working in the woods, and it was another one of those hot days. We had one of those two men chain saws. We stopped for a break. Remember we are on a hillside. The man below the tree that we had just cut down put both of his hands on the tree, and the man above the tree put his foot on the tree then stuck his axe in the tree. The man below said you cut my finger off and the other man above looked down and said dang if I hain't.

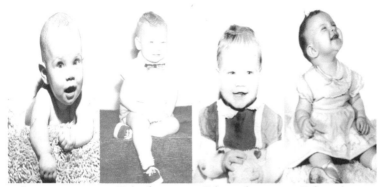

Joanna   Rickey Charlene Gloria

My dear wife gave birth to four children. We were blessed with these children. They were raised in these mountains of West Virginia. All of our children were good children. They had respect for their elders. Our children, never gave us any problems, not one ounce of trouble. My wife and I were blessed beyond compare. Now that my wife has passed away and gone, she left our children for me. They are all I have. I have the blessings of all my children. Death comes to every family, and there's nothing we can do about it. All I can tell you is to keep your house that you walk around in; In order. For we know not what hour he will come to take us to that place that we have all been waiting for. My wife (Faye) gave birth to our first daughter on January the Twenty Fourth, Nineteen Hundred and Fifty Three. Her name was Joanna Fay West. On March the Eleventh

Nineteen Hundred and Fifty Six, Faye gave birth to our only son. We named him Rickey Edward West. He was a Yankee boy. He was born in Pennsylvania when we had gone there to find work. The men at work teased me about Rickey. I told them on the second day he had already asked for the car keys. On June twenty-six Nineteen Sixty, Faye gave birth to our second daughter. We named her Myrtle Charlene West. Oh boy the family began to grow. On August the Eighth, Nineteen Hundred and Sixty Five, Faye gave birth to our third daughter Gloria Denise West. We made our living in Beeson, West Virginia. We had a small country grocery store for thirty five years. Boy, oh boy, I wish everyone in this great nation of ours would have to run a grocery store for five years. Then they would understand how hard it is to make it. My wife and I had this country store. The older people would come in and they would stay for an hour and then some. Some of the men was telling about a man here in the country. How some of these boys got together and taken the mans wagon apart and put it on top of the barn and assembled it back together. I bet the next morning there was hell to pay. Those old men would laugh and laugh. Now those men really enjoyed themselves. Those times were a lot different than the days we live in today. The difference is like daylight and dark. I remember those old people here at the store, talking about a man in one of the communities that had put a fence around some of his property. He told some people that he put up a fence that was cow proof and boy proof. Some of the men said that the old man said the wrong thing when he said boy proof, some of the young boys heard what he said, so they all got together and tore the fence down and rolled the wire up in a pile. Then they took the fence posts and put them in a nice pile. The men would come into the store and they would set and tell all of this I've been writing about. They would tell these tales and they would laugh. Then someone else would tell another tale. They would say they remember all these things and brother I would get a kick out of all this. I was taking it all in, because I thought back then that it would be wonderful to tell our children so that they would know how people enjoyed their selves. My wife wanted me to write about these things back several years ago and I have an aunt who wanted me to write about these things also.

Faye, bless her heart looked out after the store and she was also the post master. I know it was hard for her with the children to look after. As I look back, pop (soda) was one dollar and forty six cents for twenty four bottles. Candy was eighty five cents for twenty four bars and if you can believe this, we had gasoline, five gallons and two tenths for a dollar. Faye enjoyed this kind of work. She enjoyed talking to the people and all of the people loved her. I was really blessed to have her as my wife and companion. I have been blessed beyond compare. I'll tell you a little bit more about our little store that operated for thirty five years, about all of our business was credit. There were nights we would go to bed and wonder, if we were going to make it in the store business or if we were going to go under. I remember going to the bank to borrow money to live on until things got better. There was one thing my wife and I never done that was to sue anyone for a store bill. There were three other merchants in our community that couldn't say that. My wife and I just didn't have the heart to take some ones home, cattle, horses or any part of someone's land. We lost a lot of money down through the years, seems as though the Lord was with us during all of this. I think we came out on top by running our business the way we operated our store. We didn't get rich but we did have a roof over our head, clothes on our backs and food on our table. That is

one of the things that make me feel
like a good ole country boy.

This I've got to tell you about. My
wife had to go pick up two of our
children from a ball game. My oldest
and youngest daughter went with her.
When they got to the school, it was jam
packed. My wife had to go down the
street to turn around. She stopped at
the stop sign and the car stalled and
wouldn't start. She got out of the
vehicle and raised the hood on the car
when two cars pulled up beside them.
The man in the second car got out and
started arguing with the other two men
in the other car. The next thing she
knew the man shot one of the men. She
was outside her car window and told
our oldest daughter to put the youngest
in the floor. Then there was another
shot one man was killed instantly. That
night needless to say, my wife and
children were scared half out of their
wits. There was another time when Faye
and the same two children went around
to pay Faye's mother and father a visit.
As they were returning home there
came a bad hail storm. It was so bad
that the storm tore up jack. Now I can
understand about the hail storm. My
dad and one of my uncles on my
mother's side of the family were
cutting timber on my grand-father's
farm. I went over to see when dad was
going home and to beat it all I was just

a young lad. I believe it was before my mother died in nineteen thirty six. Well I had begun to believe the hail balls were going to beat the ears off my head.

There use to a place they called Shawnee Lake. Every Fourth of July this place was the main attraction for everyone. This meant a lot to us young people and some of the older people. They had picnic tables and people would take their dinner and have a wonderful time there by the lake it was surrounded by big trees for shade. They also had live music in a large building to entertain the people. I also believe there was a dance hall upstairs, but I'm not for sure. There was an old gentleman that lived in Princeton West Virginia who owned a hotel now he had hogs adjoining the lake across the road and he would bring food from the hotel to feed the hogs. There was a swimming pool and they would have life guards watching the pool at all times. They had boats that would take people for rides each one would cost twenty or twenty-five cents as well as I can remember. They had vendors like for people to buy food from. Well it was more like a circus. Now this went on all summer not just on the fourth. This was a big event for some of us that could go once a year. You know when they closed it this was one of the saddest days in Southern West Virginia. It was clean entertainment there was really no reason for closing the place. Unless the state laws were to bitter for the owner to digest, but I do know it was a wonderful place.

Faye and I really looked for-ward to Christmas when the children were small. We loved taking our children to the store, to see the excitement on their faces. Time after time we would loose one or two of the kids in the store. That's what children like to do. Let mommy find me game. On Christmas Eve, I would sit up most of the night putting toys together. It was well worth the lost sleep.

Our family and Faye's sister Dosle went to Camp Creek State Park once. We all enjoyed that day. All the children were playing. Later in the day we had a cook out.

We all went to the West Virginia State Fair, on a Friday afternoon. My son Rickey and Gary Mills was working for Darrel and myself at the time. It was pay day for the boys. Faye asked both of the boys how much money they had. They both said they didn't have any money. Needless to say, Faye gave them money.

With all the family things we have done together, Faye and I were blessed to have these four children. Faye and I both worked and toiled to give our children more than we had as children.

I only have one daughter-in-law Barbara, and I carry her high at times. I told that there was an encyclopedia salesman that had come to the house one day, wanting to sell me a set of encyclopedias. I told the man I wasn't interested, but he said every household needed a set. I then told him I didn't. I have a daughter-in-law that knows everything and if I needed to know anything I would just go and ask her.

There was a little store across from Spanishburg High School. This is where Faye attended school. A quarter would buy a hot dog, soft drink, and a bag of chips. This was the days when money went somewhere. Now days, you can't get out of town without spending a hundred dollars. That twenty dollar bill you have in your pocket isn't worth much – the young people that are being raised these days. In years to come, the twenty dollar bill will be worth even less than today. We all need to stand up and take notice. The Lord may come back before all of these years roll by.

When I was young lad growing up in Beeson West Virginia, we didn't have highways like we have today. On the Old Beckley road going into Princeton, there were times it would take an hour or longer to get from Spanishburg to Princeton. The reason for this was that the tractor trailers wasn't as high powered then as the ones we have on the highways today. Now, from Spanishburg to Princeton you can drive it in approximately fifteen or twenty minutes. There were two truck stops down by the river north of Spanishburg. One of them was owned by my uncle Leland Blankenship. He died at an early age. I don't know the cause of his death.

I worked at the saw mill, and my good friend Darrell Shrewsbury worked in the woods about all the time. I was the one who sawed the lumber. We employed a few men, but I can't recall exactly how many. I use to do a lot of work in the woods, on a dozer. Sometimes we would build roads. One time I was pushing limbs and grape vine out of the road. When I went into the woods that morning, I had taken my lunch and three Dr. Peppers (Soda) with me. I hadn't eaten or drank anything. As I was using the dozer, a limb jerked up and knocked me out. When I came too, I was lying back over the fuel tank of the dozer. I climbed off the dozer, and I had to lie down on the ground. I was as sick as a horse, if you know how sick a horse gets. I got up to go where the other men were working. I had to stop a lot of times because I was so sick. When I finally got to the top of the hill, I sat down again and began waving at the other workers. I couldn't yell; I could hardly talk. My son finally saw me. He got into the truck and took me to the hospital. I had a very large concussion to the head. Now I'm going to stop and tell you something that goes along with this story. There was a fellow that came into the store that my wife and I operated. His body was weak and frail. He was very feeble. He said to me that he thought he was going to die, I told him; sir, there is nothing wrong with a man dying. He replied; I have a family and I don't want to leave them. Well guess what happened. My son and I passed the church about three o'clock that evening, and they were having a funeral there, which my wife was attending. My son asked me if I wanted him to stop and get Faye (my wife). I told my son no, to go on. I was thinking of getting to the hospital. I thought I was going to die. Now just take a guess as to whom the funeral service was for. It was the weak frail man I had told that there was nothing wrong with a man dying. Now you see that big fat piece of meat in our mouths called the tongue can get us in a lot of trouble. I guess we should stop and think what the Lord warned us about our tongue. It's the most evil part of our body. I try to put my trust in the lord. By now you can realize that I do.

While I was in the saw mill business we had a man working for us. He and I were working at the mill one Saturday. We were using a five horse power drill to drill holes thru four by eight collars, for the mines. The big drill had us both down in the floor. It threw him behind the cut off saw and I rode the storm out. That thing was beating the devil out of me. Finally the cord broke. I looked over at my buddy and he was still laying there. I said are you OK? He said; I don't know. I'll just have to get up and check and see if I'm hurt. Once we had sent him to the woods to cut timber. One man was cutting timbers and another man was pulling the timbers with a horse. The one man talked about the drill working on me and him. About that time, a limb fell out of a tree and hit him in the head. It knocked him out. When he came to his senses, he said; Lord, I'll never see my wife again.

Once I was hauling coal at Arista, West Virginia. There was a new mines being opened, and I was to get the first load from them. I pulled up, but they didn't have a load ready. I was told that as soon as they put a collar and two timbers up they would let me know. Now let me remind you that this is where coal had already been stripped and mined. They were going under a high wall. To continue, there were three men setting the timbers and a collar. I looked over and there was a man in the middle trying to push that collar up by himself, I started over to help him, but something told me to go ahead and eat my sandwich and then I would be ready to go when they were ready to start loading. I went back to the truck and unwrapped my sandwich. Lo and behold, I looked up and that whole mountain was coming down on that poor man. If I hadn't gone to the truck for my sandwich I would have been under there with him. Now people, if you hear a little voice, take heed to his talking. The reason he didn't take me along with that man, I had heeded to that little voice I heard.

One time a good friend of mine and I were working at a coal mine called Crane Creek. This friend of mine was much older than I, but he was a wonderful person to be around. Just to hear him talk would blow your socks off. You can figure how my day at work was. He was a fun person to be around. He rode to work with me. On Monday morning after we were paid on Friday, his wife would put his ride money in an envelope and he would give it to me. There was a family that lived on top of the mountain. They had three young girls, and they looked to be sixteen or seventeen years old. They were good looking girls. As we came past their house on our way to work, my good friend was looking at them one evening. I told him; oh yea, I saw you winking at those girls. He replied there was a damn gnat in my eye. I said; you wait until I tell your wife, you'll think a gnat. Our work place was around the strip where they had taken a dozer and moved the dirt off and got the coal. We would go under the ground with a wheel barrow to move the coal out. I remember one day I was digging coal above the middle man (as they called it). It wasn't anything but rock. We would go on all the time as we were digging coal. I was mocking someone. I don't recall who it was, but I hit my finger between the rocks and pick handle. I mean brother, I done it in good. He laughed and laughed. He said; damn-it maybe you'll mock someone else now.

I remember coming thru the town of Matoaka, West Virginia. My friend said there is the five and ten cent store, and there's nothing in there under a dollar. I had a Nineteen Forty Plymouth that wouldn't pull the hat off of your head. He said; I bet you a dollar you can't go over the top of Matoaka Mountain in high gear. It was a long mountain. I'd go up the mountain in second gear and just before we would get to the top I'd go into high gear. Then I would say give me my dollar. He would say, you don't get no dollar from me. You came all the way up that mountain in second gear.

I can remember when another good friend of mine had a saw mill. This man lived in a little shack beside the road. I would go to the saw mill and we would shoot the breeze. We had wonderful times together, although he was much older than I. He would always carry a lot of money with him, most of it in one hundred dollar bills. He would take it out of his pocket and laugh about it, because he knew I didn't have a dime to my name. All of this was before he married. After he married the hundred dollar bills were down the drain, much to his disappointment.

I knew another man that I worked with. He lived in a cellar like thing. We were working at a punch mines, and we had to use a wheel barrow to wheel the coal out. One morning, I went to work, and the man didn't show up. I couldn't work without someone else being there. I went back home, and then went to his house to check on him. I knocked and knocked at that cellar door, but he wouldn't answer. Later that after-noon the police went to his shack and hauled him out of there. Come to find out, he had broken into the school house in the community and cleaned everything out, that there was in the school house. I was out of a job again, because he was mine certified and I wasn't. When things are going bad or good, I am still a good ole country boy. Now how do you like those apples?

Dillard Lawrence Kenny Faye Ernest

The Happy Four Quartet
Lawrence Dillard Arvin Ernest Harold
Faye

The Happy Four

I was a lead singer with a group of men and my loving wife was the piano player. We sang for twenty one years and we saw many people come to the Altar while we were singing. Now brother that makes you and the whole group happy. Now you can see why he didn't take me with that man. That's enough to make me rejoice in my savior. There are so many things we can rejoice in. He gets us out of bed each morning. We can raise up each morning. Look out and see the robins playing in the yard and the beautiful sun rise and know that he has given us another day. In the evening he lets us see the beautiful sun set as it sets off a beautiful glow over the clouds. We can see back in the west the army jets climbing up and the jet fuel being burned off. Now brothers and sisters, that's what it takes to be a Good Ole Country Boy.

I have written a few songs, and some have been recorded and some have not. Once there was a lady at our church who was at a local grocery store on Christmas Eve. This lady was knocked down, and broke her hip. Due to her broken hip; she was out of church for a long while. One Sunday, one of the Deacons came to me and asked if I would write a song about her. I told him that my wife and I would do our very best. This was a wonderful old lady and she had a rough time in her life. She was ninety years old, or maybe a little older. When she came back to church the deacon and I got up in front of the congregation and sang the song I had written about her. She really got a kick out of that. My wife and I really had fun doing that. We did the best that we could do.

We went to church once to sing. It was in the summer months and it was really hot. We were all dressed up, and when we got up to sing, it began to get hotter and hotter. The church was full of people. I was the lead singer of the group and it seemed as if when the words came out of my mouth they would come back and hit me in the face. I just stopped singing, and when I stopped all the others stopped singing also. I looked at all of them and said; there is something wrong with us or there is something wrong with this church. The pastor never said a word, and when we left he didn't say thank you or come back or anything. As we were driving home, we just knew we would never go back to that church, but after about a month had passed, the church called and asked us to come back and sing for them again. We went back. When we sang our first song, people began to fill the Altar. The pastor told us later that there wasn't anything wrong with you fellows. It was what was wrong with the church.

My wife and I had a lot of good days in the fifty-two and a half years we were together. We have a wonderful family. As I told you before, we

were blessed with four children. I also have two sons-in-law, one daughter-in-law, five grandchildren and five great-grandchildren. Someone asked Faye one day, how she could put up with that man, meaning myself. Her reply was quite simple. I wouldn't have him any other way. I would joke a lot with her. With all these years we were together she and I had love in our life, which needs to be in every family's life. Love in a family makes all the difference in ones home, along with God leading us.

I don't want anyone thinking I am an angel. Oh I am a far cry from that. There used to be a joke I would tell people about when we lived in Pennsylvania. I told some of the people there that I had bought my wife Faye a new washing machine. Our neighbor Mr. Dan was out in the yard when Faye came out of the house. He asked her how she liked her new washing machine. Faye replied that she loved it, but when she got in it to take a bath, the paddles just about beat her to death. From there, good news travels fast. Another time I told some people that Faye and I gotten into a fight and I had her down on her knees begging to me. I was under the bed and she was down there saying come out from there you coward you. You see that was one of my bad days, we had some. In the early sixties, we had some cattle at my grandmother's place. I had talked Faye into going with me to feed. I had an old jeep truck I drove around in. The jeep didn't have a brake one on it. As we were coming back from feeding, I ran off of the road. When we came to a stop, the jeep was ready to turn over. I asked Faye, why didn't you tell me that I was running out of the road? She said I wasn't driving.

136

The church had taken me under their wing in the year of the Lord Nineteen Hundred and Seventy Nine. Faye went to church many years before I went. Faye had done many things for the church before I attended. Faye couldn't play the piano, but she had a book or two, and with the help of the good Lord, she learned to play. One Sunday, the pastor had started leading the songs and made a smart remark about the whole thing. In a few days, her name was taken off of the church book. Before this the young people of the church wanted to have a hotdog sale for something going on for the youth group. Faye and Wanda Tyree made all of the hotdogs and the young people delivered them. Those two women worked like dogs. Then someone in my family got up on Sunday and said that they didn't believe the money had all been turned in to the church. You know that someone needs to tell these things. Now I will tell you about my experience at Beeson Chapel Church. On one Sunday the same man that I spoke about above, became a deacon of the church. He and another man were standing in front of the congregation as the people in the church were giving them their hand in fellowship. I didn't go up to shake their hand. So some of the members had said that I was mad because the church hadn't chosen me as a deacon. First you must have a desire to be in office for deacon, and that I did not have. I could have told them why, but they would not have believed me. They thought they had my number already. This same man I spoke of above had stopped in front of my house and pulled one of the most awful fits you have ever seen or heard. Now, why would I want to give him the hand of fellowship? Once the church wanted to do something to the outside of the church walls. Brother Delp asked me to get something going, about form stone on the walls. I told them I would get a man's name, that could do the job and I did. The church agreed for this man to do the job. No-one from the church knew this mans name or where he was from. This man had worked on the walls a couple of days, then didn't show back up, so I called his home and asked to speak with Bill. His wife informed me that he had a heart attack. He had his wife to tell me, that the church needed to find someone else to do the job. One Saturday evening, they had a business meeting. I told them what Bill's wife had said, and then they voted to send a bunch of men to find out why he wasn't working. One of the men said I was beholding to the church. I went home and called Bill. He said he didn't want them to come. Therefore I wouldn't give them his name, his phone number, nor tell them where he lived. Later on I told the Pastor his home address. They went there and the pastor said to me; he told us the same thing that you told the church.

Once the church was holding a revival, Brother Delp wanted the pastor, my Dad and I to come to the Altar and pray with him. The next day, the word was out in the community. That it should have been my relative up there not Lawrence West. When services started the next evening, and someone else wanted prayer, I got up out of my seat and headed for the front door. As I walked out that door the Lord called, what do you think you are doing? Are you running from me? At that point, I had a change of heart and mind, so I turned around and went back into the church, like a little whipped puppy and I took my seat. Now you see a poor little ole country boy can take instructions from a higher power.

I always did like plays and had the opportunity to be in a lot of them. At the church I attended, I once played the part of a professor. The people in one of the rooms where we come out of was holding the door so there would be a small crack in the door, so those in the back could hear the one out front of the church and what they were saying. They all were scared. I was sitting in a big chair with a suit and tie on. At this point I began to think I had gotten away from being a good ole country boy and became one of those city slickers. Well, anyway one of the lady's at the church was playing a part as one of my daughters and she came by and said daddy are you nervous? And I said as nervous as a long tail cat in a room full of rocking chair. That wasn't my part at all. That church was packed with people and you couldn't hear anything for awhile. I tell you right now those people laughed and laughed for quite a while. And the people in the back said if he can get away with it we can. It seems though I broke the knot that turned the camel loose. The people in the community loved those plays and they looked forward each and every Christmas. We had people there in that church that could really play their parts good, and we also had a church choir that could sing along with the best. We had a play one Christmas and I played a part of a thief. I would get their necklaces off from their neck and they wouldn't know it. In one scene I was a pick pocket. I sat down on my hand and bent my finger back the wrong way. There was a doctor there and he pulled my finger and I began to holler. Then I passed out and fell on the floor broadsided. Out as cold as a cucumber and one of the lady's thought something had happened to me. She about had a heart attack, now I'm getting back to being a Good Ole Country Boy.

I have done a lot of joking in my life time, and you know that it's better than someone walking around with a long face that would look like a mule face. I would pass on the jokes I have heard from other people. I will write one I heard from someone else that was told to m. This one I heard about a church going to have a revival. An elderly lady lived up the road from the church she lived by herself and she told her pastor one Sunday morning that she was afraid to walk the road after dark. The pastor told her to come on and if anyone attacks you, you quote Acts two, thirty eight. Well guess what? Two old boys jumped out on her one night, and she quoted Acts two, thirty eight. One of the boys broke to run and the other one asked why are you running? Didn't you hear what that lady said, that she had an axe and two thirty- eights.

Now here is another one. A lady went to church one Sunday night and asked the church to pray that something might happen to the beer joint down the road from her house. They all went back to church on Wednesday night. Some of the church people said well sister so and so your prayers were answered. The lady said I like to put legs on my prayers, the beer joint burned down.

Here is another story about a good ole country boy. One night as I lay in my bed, in the early hours I had a vision or a dream, whatever you would like to call it. I saw the face of Jesus or I thought it was him. That will be for you to sort out. He was up there in the bright light. I mean it was beautiful and I was in a dark valley. When I awakened, I thought the Lord had come to take his children home with him. I'm talking about the sheep, even though he is the shepherd of the flock, and I wasn't ready. I was sleeping by my self that night, so I got up out of the bed. I first checked on my wife. She was in her bed. Then I went to check the children's beds and they were all there. I had been having some miserable days; I was thinking that I had read in the Bible that if you had a dream of this sort, that you were not to tell anyone. Later on I went over to where we had some men working, cleaning off a slate dump for a coal company. One of the men we had working was older than I, so I called for him to come to me. It was very hot, so we sat down on a log and I began to tell him about what had happened. He looked at me and said, my dad had a dream like that, and about two weeks after he had the dream, he died. Now all of that sure made me feel much better.

Here's a little joke I told some folks one time. I said I went to town one day to get me a pair of shoes and I took my half brother with me. When we got out of the car, down the street from the shoe store my half brother said he would wait on the street where the car was. I went on to the shoe store and I told the man what I wanted. He looked at me with the most unusual look on his face, and he said to me if you can show me a man that is uglier than you I'll give you a pair of shoes free of charge. So I went to the door and whistled for my brother Acie and I got me a pair of shoes free of charge. Now you see it pays to be a good ole country boy at times.

I must tell you about the pastor of the church I attend today. We have a dinner at the fellowship hall once a month. He had been there about a year or maybe more and I thought it would be appropriate to have him come up front and explain a few things about himself. I first called him to come up and he just looked at me out of the corner of his eyes. Then I asked him again, and he came that time. I put my arm around his shoulder and I said church, you are blessed to have this man as your pastor. He has a big and good heart, and he will fall for anything. Then I began to tell them, that I was climbing a long ladder to see Saint Peter. I got about half way up the ladder, and I became tired and couldn't go any farther. Then here come brother Don. He asked what I was doing. I told him I was on my way up the ladder to see Saint Peter, but I couldn't make it. Don said I am on my way to see Saint Peter also, so you get on my back and I will carry you up. When we got up Saint Peter's door, he said Lawrence, it's good to see you old buddy, just tie your donkey up and come on in. I've just been joking, our pastor is a good man

Larlyn Foley

There used to be a couple of men that came into the store that my wife operated, frequently. These two men could have made a movie, by just acting natural. One mans name was Larlyn Foley. It was in the middle of winter, and Larlyn had just come in from work, where he operated a large dozer on a strip job. I asked him, if he was doing OK? He said hell no, I've got a block of ice under each knee cap. That was a pretty amazing story. Doesn't that sound good? Once, Larlyn's wife had sent him to the store to get a new stove. The stove turned over. It just happened, that my wife and Larlyn's wife was going somewhere together.

They met Larlyn on the road and stopped. Larlyn told them that the stove had turned over. Larlyn's wife said; that is just like a man, they can't do a damn thing right. Boy oh boy did that set off a war of words, and my wife was caught up in the middle. I bet at that point and time that she didn't feel like a good ole country girl. Here's a good little tale that I have had a lot of fun with. Larlyn and his wife had been out all day one Sunday, and darkness had fallen, Larlyn had to go out and split wood. He heard his dog out in the woods barking, so he went to the dog, and found that he had a opossum treed. One of his neighbors (Wilber) came over to where the dog had the opossum treed. Wilbur was two sheets in the wind. Wilbur asked Larlyn, What have you got up the tree and Larlyn said, I have got a opossum up there. Wilbur said, I am going to climb that tree and shake the opossum out. Then you are going to get down on your hands and knees and kill the opossum, just like a dog, or you are going to have to fight me. Larlyn said; Wilbur, I know you are a big man, but I will fight you before I fight that damn opossum.

I like to joke and I have all down through the years, out at our church where I and my wife attended until she passed away and now I just go alone.

We started going in 1981. This past fall there was an eighty nine year old lady that wasn't at church one Sunday morning and she had been going there for years. Well no one knew where she was. We all got up in the choir and they were still commenting about her and I happen to know where she was, I told them she was down south some where she was laying out on the beach. Boy oh boy was she upset after she found out about it. She told me I owed the church an apology for lying to the church, so I told some one I don't stay where I can't joke. I hope I'm not wrong, but I don't think the lord wants us to go around with a frown on our face.

Well I guess I get a lot from my dad. He was a cracker jack. He was a preacher and he didn't tell dirty jokes. You see you don't have to tell dirty jokes, there are too many clean jokes. I heard him telling some people that there wasn't one difference between my stepmother and a woodpecker. That the woodpecker sets and pecks, and she would set and nod. I remember one time there was a bear coming up to a trash dump up a little dirt road above Springton, West Virginia. My stepmother asked my dad who you could see to get permission to see the bear, she said her and a friend wanted to go see it, and my dad told her she would have to call the mayor of

Matoaka to get permission to see the bear. Well she called the mayor that day while dad was at work. When dad got home that evening my stepmother was fit to whip a bear. Another time my stepmother had some young chickens and they or some of them began to lay eggs. My stepmother was telling people how good her chickens were laying eggs so come to find out my dad was buying eggs and putting them in the hen's nests. One time he would buy one dozen of eggs and some days he would buy two dozen.

I went to the doctor. Well I go to him all the time, but he wanted me to go to another doctor for he couldn't write the prescriptions that I needed. So my oldest daughter Joanna and I went to see that doctor. We walked into the office and asked for the doctor we were looking for, and she said here she is go with her. As we were walking up the hallway she said the last door there is my office. I stopped and looked at the door and what I saw liked to blew my socks off. Over the door was psychiatrist. I stopped and said what am I doing here? She said go in and get a seat and we'll find out what your doing here. She sunk up in a big old chair. We talked a while and she done away with a lot of jelly beans. Then she began to ask questions. The first one was, did you ever think about suicide?

And I said, who told you? I got this line from my half sister. She always comes up with stuff like this. Another question she asked was what roll do you think you play in life? I said I think my roll in life is to make people laugh, and she said how is that? I told her that all people had to do was to just look at me and they would laugh. You see hearing those things I have been relating to you makes me feel good, and that makes me think I'm a Good Ole Country Boy.

I go to the veteran's hospital all the time. I chew tobacco and have for years. The doctor rides me about it all the time. I had an appointment with the eye doctor and someone in his office asked when was I going to stop that chewing? I said doc, when am I going to die? Now I know this is a nasty habit and I won't encourage teenagers to take up such habits as chewing or smoking. When you have a habit like this it's hard to just stop. I soon will be Seventy Six. I guess if it was going to get me it would have done got me. My wife used to say it's the first thing in the morning and the last thing at night. And if by any chance you read this, take my advice, don't start for it's not good for you.

As I am writing this, I hear them on television talking about the shooting that happened in Blacksburg Virginia that killed all those college children. That was a shame folks. We are living in a different world than a lot of us were brought up in. We as Americans just don't know where we are safe. We are living in a crazy world and it doesn't look like it's going to get any better. When I grew up you didn't have to lock your doors at night or when they left home.

I will now tell you a little about our government, and the people that served us as a whole. I hear people on television these days, trashing our president. I can remember as a child, that if you said anything about our president and it got out into the public, what had been said, there would be someone looking for you. I was raised under some of Hoover's administration, but not for long, then Franklin Roosevelt was elected. During all of this, times were hard, and people didn't have much. After these hard times, people had respect for their president. My, oh my how things have changed. Today our Senators will get on television and blast our president, and a lot of these Senators know better than that, because a lot of then came up in life like I did. It's no wonder that our president can't get anything done, and it's playing into the terrorist hands. They know that they have the people in this good USA divided and this is what is going to bring old America to her knees. In this good ole USA, people have forgotten God and the sad part is I believe our leaders have forgotten God also. The Bible says that a nation that forgets or turns from God will be cast out into outer darkness. Now let us step back and focus on what I have just written. Now people we must remind ourselves just where we are going. When I was growing up here in Beeson, I was reminded often by the hickory switch, and they were in every corner of the house. They knew how to use them also. I love to sit in my lazy chair and watch what is going on in the world. Recently a hurricane called Katrina came thru Louisiana. The more I look at this thing, the more I think about it, this drives me up a wall. All of these people stayed there waiting for the government to come and bail them out. Well folks, I'm about as bright as a burnt out light bulb, but you see our government can't even spend our tax money. We send it to them. They take the money that we pay them each year, and then they send it over seas and just blow it--now, this to both democrats and republicans. They show these people on television. You don't see any of them working. You see them all on the streets going and coming, and they can hardly pass one another. I will tell you one thing. If the people out in the mid-west would not farm for two years, the whole world would starve to death. Now I talked about Katrina early on and about how bright I was. If I had been there, and I had seen all of that water coming in, I would have had my family on my back and we would have left town. With all of the buses down there it seem to me like the mayor should have gotten those buses on the move hauling those people out of there, instead they put all of the blame on our president. This is the most outrageous thing I have ever heard of. I wonder if the mayor would walk out on the street and fart, would he blame our president for that. People in the good ole USA seem to think that the people from West Virginia are weak and under educated. That we just don't know what is going on in the world. Just look around and have another thought. Some folks in West Virginia are as wise as some of the wise old owls that are in these mountains. This is why I am proud to be a Good Ole Country Boy.

Do you know what is better than being a Good Ole Country Boy, it's being an American--in a land where the milk and honey grows. We can look around, and see a lot of good people. Sometimes we wonder why bad things happen to good people. You can just look around again and see all the things that God has made for us to look at--the beauty that he has given us to look at.

I have a motor home. I enjoy taking trips. My wife and I used to go to the Smokey Mountains quite frequently. The travels are not as enjoyable without her. I tried to get my good friend Garfield Kirk to take a trip with me. Garfield is the funeral director at Bailey Kirk Funeral Home in Princeton, West Virginia. Garfield was unable to accompany me on this trip. He had staff out on vacation.

I have been blessed in this lifetime. I will soon be seventy six years old. I have defeated cancer two times. I do have some medical problems, but I am still able to care for myself and travel when I want to. I have a wood working shop I work in a lot. I enjoy making furniture and different things. I have a family and relatives that love me and can be depended on. Not everyone can make that statement. I love the Lord for blessing me and my life so much.

I ride down to the Smokey Mountains quiet often. I was thinking about a trip I took. The trees in the fall of the year the colors are beautiful. People would come from mile around to see the colors of the trees. They would come to see the Christmas lights, oh, they are all wonderful to look at and enjoy. I went the other day to Morgantown and up by Fairmont as I was driving up I-79 north, I began to compare the woods and mountains. Although, the mountains are higher in the Smokies, the mountains of West Virginia will be so pretty while driving on I-79 in the fall of the year. You can see for miles as you are driving. The Christmas lights in pigeon forge are beautiful. But the Christmas lights in Bluefield City Park, are beyond compare. Bluefield comes out on top again. Folks you have got to see them, to believe it.

Yesterday as I was crossing over the Great Smokey Mountains. As I was coming back from the top of the Smokey Mountain, the traffic had come to a halt. I thought there must be a bad wreck. I saw people running down the highway. The traffic began to move a little bit. I saw people standing there looking up on the mountain. I began looking up the mountain also. I experienced something I had never seen before. There were black bears on the hillside. This was something I had never witnessed before. They were so beautiful, so pretty and black and clean. I let my windows down in the car so I could hear the water running over the rocks and the falls, the large trees shading everywhere. You could feel the cool breeze all around and I was thinking this is Mother Nature at her best. The birds singing their song, it might not be songs to us, but I'm sure it was to them. It's amazing how God made all of the creatures. God made men and women not a one of us look alike. We might be able to count the stars if we had a big calculator and plenty of time on our hands. We can gaze at the moon, but we can't gaze to long at a time or we might fall over something and get hurt bad. We may see the sun come up and marvel at the beauty of it. The clouds that we see that is full of beautiful colors, we may see the storms come and go, and see the damage it has done, or we may see the rainbow with such a beautiful arc, but I have not heard of anyone finding a pot of gold at the end of it anywhere. God created all this beauty for our eyes.

Lyrics to the songs I have written:

When Satan Took Jesus On The Mountain Top

1. When Satan he took Jesus on the mountain top, and showed him all the kingdoms, and said this can all be yours, then Jesus soon replied get the behind, that Satan turned away to leave for awhile.

2. Satan will deceive you and tell you a lot of lies, lead you through this world and you'll lose your home on high, just keep your eyes on Jesus, no matter what Satan does, you'll never regret it when you reach that home above.

_____chorus:

So Jesus is our savior, he shines all the time, and if we follow Jesus we'll leave Satan far behind, just keep your eyes on heaven and that sweet home you'll see, for Jesus is our savior, and he shines all the time, yes Jesus is our savior and he shines all the time, and he shines, shines, all the time.

Let's Go Back To Bethel

1. When we walk down by the river, by the river that flows from God's mighty throne, there we'll see all our friends and loved ones, that we once known, they will greet us with a holy kiss, and bid us come on in, so let us all go back to bethel, where it all began.

2. Our friends will take us for a tour down the street of purest gold, those mansions there will seem so beautiful and pure with our names written above the door, and the angels will be singing like we never heard before, so let us all go back to bethel where it all began.

____chorus:

Let us all go back to bethel, let us go with a smile and grin, let us renew our vows at bethel the place where our first love began, let us kneel and pray at bethel, and let our hearts be with joy, so let us all go back to bethel, where it all began.

Walking with Jesus

1. I think of Moses' as he traveled this land, how Jesus led him to the promise land, he guided him daily as he said he would do, God's grace is sufficient for me and for you.

2. There's a mansion in glory that I can go to, and he will give me a crown all shiny and new, if you will let Jesus come in to your heart, a mansion and crown is waiting for you.

3. Come walk on the streets that are made of pure gold, a place where we will never grow old, where the gates are pearl, and white as snow, where there shall be beauty and rest for your soul.

____chorus:

I'm walking with Jesus, both day and night, he's leading me gently, to that heavenly light, where there shall be beauty and rest for my soul, for he is my savior, he has made me whole.

I Heard An Angel Speak

1. One day I heard an angel speak, he said I could be saved, if only I'd believe in God and do his will each day, I promised him that I would do, the things he'd have me to do, and the angel left me and went away.

2. Then the angel reappeared and this is what he said, do you remember the beautiful flowers that bloom each spring in the month of May, if you will read your Bible sing and pray, you to can be like a flower in that beautiful garden some day.

____chorus:

Yes I heard that angel speak, while I was down by the brook, it made me feel so afraid that I broke into tears, when I fell upon my knees, and there began to pray, the Lord above heard my prayers, on that very day.

My Levi and I

1. Now you may take my name, and slander it around, and you may take my family and bury them in the ground. You may take my home and burn it all down, but there are some things I beg of you.

(chorus)

2. You may take my car and run it out of gas. You may take my land I lived. On in the past, you may take my shirt and drag it in the dirt, but there some things I beg of you

(chorus)

3. Now you may take my jet and fly it out of town. You may take my money and throw it around. You may take my coon hound and haul him away, but there is some things I beg of you.

____chorus:

Please don't take my Levi I chewed on so long, and please don't take my vitamins that I depended on. Please don't take my wife she's the joy of my life, they all have been around so long.

Grandma Got Run Over by a Stranger

1. Now grandma gets excited when Christmas comes around, she is planning on the children come riding into town, there she will build those pumpkin pies, and set them by the stove, by ned's she's a happy woman when Christmas comes once more.

2. Now grandma rode her junker down to the general store, to get some mistletoe to hang on the door, and when that joker knocked her down mistletoe went all around, and they gave her some holiday spirits and rolled her out of town.

____chorus:

grandma got run over by a stranger, down at the general store, as she was on her way from the checkout counter, some folks said she had to much eggnog, but as for me, I believe she missed the door and fell on the floor.

West's songs recorded on gospel tape

Tuesday, January 2, 2001 A-5

Song writing could become new career for 69-year-old

By KATHY KISH
of the Daily Telegraph staff

Lawrence West is a testimony to the fact that it is never too late to start something new. At 69 years old he is just breaking into the song writing business. And he didn't even take an interest in music until 12 years ago.

"I was 47 years old before I started singing," West said. "I went to church one day and the choir leader was gone. They said 'we've got a choir leader' and they pointed at me. I've been singing ever since."

Two gospel songs West wrote, titled "Lets all go back Bethel" and "I Heard An Angel Speak" are included on a tape that was recently released by Hilltop Records. The tape is called "In The Beginning."

West said the tape is produced as a way to market newly written songs to professional singers.

West retired from West Grocery in Beeson about seven years ago after 35 years. He started writing about five years ago.

"I've only written about eight or 10 songs," West said. "I just retired and I don't have a whole lot to do. I just happened to think 'Well that would just be a good thing to do.' So I wrote six or eight gospel songs and wrote a couple country songs.

"I just picked up a pencil and paper one day and thought I'm gonna write a song," he said. "I Heard An Angel Speak' was the first one I wrote. The second one I wrote, Jesus Shines all the time. Hill Top wants to put on another tape. I'm supposed to get royalties out of it but I won't know until the last of April how much I'll get. They pay royalties on a quarterly

basis... whatever they sell to commercial or private buyers or whatever."

In spite of his laid-back attitude about the reasons he wrote the songs, West did take care to guard his writing by sending the songs to the to the Library of Congress in Washington, D.C. for copyrights.

"I sing them on a tape and send the tape, then about a week to 10 days later you get a receipt back from where they received it," he said. "I'll probably get the copyrights in five or six months."

Writing songs has become a family affair for West, his wife and daughter. He writes them, his daughter, JoAnna Shrewsbury, wrote the music for the first few, and his wife plays the tune on the piano while he sings it.

Both he and his wife are humble about their talents though.

"The lord is the reason we do anything," Lenettice said.

"The lord gives us the talent to do with," said West.

West said he has been the lead singer in a gospel quartet called the Happy Four Quartet for about 20 years now. The other members of the quartet include Dillard Lyle (tenor) Ernest Lyle (bass singer) and Arvin Cecil (baritone). Lenettice plays the piano for them.

"We go to sing at different churches," West said. "On Labor Day before last we sang down at Pigeon Forge at a gospel sing."

West said the group has recorded three tapes of well-known gospel songs.

While most of the songs West writes and sings are gospel, he also has a sense of humor.

"I wrote one country song called 'My Levi and I.' It's

about chewing tobacco. It's a comical song that's got Viagra and all that kind of stuff in it," he said with a laugh.

He noted that he also wrote a song about a true incident that happened with a shopping cart in a local grocery store called "Grandma Got Run Over By A Stringer."

Lawrence West has two of his songs recorded on 'In The Beginning.'

Staff photo by Kathy Kish

My beautiful wife, Faye West

I would like to tell you a little bit about my wife when she was on her death bed. She was in her right mind right up to the last second of her life. All the people that knew her knew that she was the same Ole Faye everyday of her life. Faye had been diagnosed with liver cancer, just two weeks prior to her death. Faye wanted to be at home, so myself, our four children, Joanna, Rickey, Charlene and Denise stayed with her twenty four hours a day, along with our grandson Michael, daughter-in-law Barbara and Faye's Niece Linda, until she went to be with our Lord. Faye had told me a couple of weeks before she passed on, that she loved me, but that she loved the lord more. Although she endured a lot of pain, she would raise her hands to heaven and praise the Lord. Our son Rickey had told his mother, that he was going to hold her hand and be there with her, and when she got to the pearly gates, to squeeze his hand; and as she drew her last breathe, she gave his hand the slightest squeeze. There were so many people that came into our home to do what ever we needed done. My Brother-in-law said to me; do you see all those cars up and down the road, don't that tell you something; I said yes it does. It tells me that Faye has a lot of friends, people that really love her. Brother and Sister Arnold Akers was with our family from early in the morning to late in the evening. These are true friends that are with you through thick and thin, Brother Arnold Akers is a preacher. He goes way back. He has served our country, worked in the coal mines and he was a school teacher, which taught most of our children. One day they were here and Sister Akers was running the vacuum cleaner. Someone said she doesn't need to be doing that, and I replied, you better not try to take that vacuum cleaner from her. Brother Akers also took part in the funeral services for my wife.

Arnold and Drema Akers

Lawrence and Linda Mills

Lawrence and Evelyn Atwood

Our neighbors, down below us was with us all through Faye's illness. Their names were Lawrence and Linda Mills. Faye was Linda's Aunt. Linda and Faye were always close, although Faye was her Aunt, they were pretty close in age and they grew up together. You know, when people come into your home like I have been speaking of, you know you are blessed. Linda would stay about every night, and help with the care given to Faye and support the children with anything she could. Lawrence and Linda have been a true blessing to this family; even today they keep a watch out over me, to make certain that everything is OK. My sister and brother-in-law; Lawrence and Evelyn Atwood also played a large part in our sorrow. They were with our family everyday, and they found out just how close our family was, just those good ole poor mountain folks. There was two of our good ole friends that Faye and I had sang with for twenty one years. After all that time together, singing, practicing and going from church to church, you know we had to be good friends. Their names were Dillard Lyle and Arvin Cecil. These two gentlemen were at our home everyday while Faye was ill. They would bring in food and offer their friendship daily, as well as our pastor, Justin Farley and his wife Sherry. Justin preached the funeral service for my wife. The Sunday following my wife's burial, Justin resigned from the church as pastor.

The owners of L&M Market in Lashmeet, WV; Lloyd and Mary Bennett brought in loads of groceries to our house. Mary told me that night if you only need a bag of ice, I will see that you get it. If I am unable to bring it I will send it by someone else. Now people if that's not friendship I don't know what is. My sister's Eilean and Christine and their husbands were always there for us also. There were so many people that came to our home to offer their help, friendship, love, and sympathy. The church people were great about stopping by, to offer any assistance they could. I can't recall everyone by name, because there was so many, but each and everyone was appreciated, for their concern and friendship. Hospice of the two Virginias was wonderful. Nurse Kay made sure that Faye was comfortable and had everything that she needed. I would recom-mend Hospice to anyone, who is in their last days of life. Now, things like this is what makes me feel Blessed to be a Good Ole Country Boy, and have the friends that I have.

168

In Memory

Faye West

BEESON – Faye Peyton West, 69, of 4118 Beeson Road, Beeson, died Friday, Aug. 6, 2004 in the year of our Lord 2004 at home surrounded by her loving family, husband, Lawrence; three daughters, Joanna Shrewsbury and her husband Arnold and their son Michael, and Charlene Sexton and her daughter Brandy and Denise Farmer; son, Rickey West and his wife Barbara; niece, Linda Mills; and preacher, Arnold Akers. Born Dec. 10, 1934 at Spanishburg, she was the daughter of the late Douglas Peyton and Lou Annie Peyton.

Mrs. West was loved by everyone. She was a wonderful wife, mother, grandmother and great-grandmother. She was greatly loved by her children, grandchildren and great-grandchildren. She loved family get togethers and always loved going to the farmer's market. Her grandson, Michael Shrewsbury and niece Linda Mills lovingly and faithfully were by her side until the end. Faye was a faithful piano player for 20 years for the Happy Four Quartet. She was postmaster for 38 years at Beeson from Oct. 31, 1959 until March 31, 1997. She was a member of NARP. She attended Cooks Chapel since 1981.

Survivors include her husband of 52 years, Lawrence West; three daughters, Joanna Shrewsbury and her husband Arnold of Beeson, Charlene Sexton of Black Oak and Denise Farmer and her husband Johnny of Matoaka; one son, Rickey West and his wife Barbara of Beeson; five grandchildren and five great-grandchildren; one sister, Flossie Lay of Ohio; and one brother, Ray Peyton of Pennsylvania.

Funeral services will be conducted tonight at 7 p.m., at the Rowland H. Bailey Funeral Chapel of the Bailey-Kirk Funeral Home in Princeton with Rev. Justin Farley, Arnold Akers and Rev. Randolph Dishner officiating.

Interment and graveside service will be at 10 a.m., Tuesday, Aug. 10, 2004 at Roselawn Memorial Gardens in Princeton. Pallbearers will be Arvin Cecil, Ernest Lyle, Dillard Lyle, Michael Shrewsbury, J.W. Farmer and Danny Shrewsbury. Friends attending the graveside service are asked to meet at the funeral home by 9:30 a.m. on Tuesday.

Friends may call today from 6 p.m., until service hour at the Bailey-Kirk Funeral Home in Princeton.

Here is a poem that my granddaughter in-law gave to my family when Faye passed away that I would like to share with you. I am not certain who the author is, but it is filled with beauty.

A LIMB FALLEN

A LIMB HAS FALLEN FROM THE FAMILY TREE
I KEEP HEARING A VOICE THAT SAYS "GRIEVE NOT FOR ME"
REMEMBER THE BEST TIMES,
THE LAUGHTER, THE SONG, THE GOOD LIFE I LIVED WHILE I WAS STRONG
CONTINUE MY HERITAGE, I'M COUNTING ON YOU
KEEP SMILING AND SURELY THE SUN WILL SHINE THROUGH
MY MIND IS AT EASE, MY SOUL IS AT REST
REMEMBER ALL HOW I TRULY WAS BLESSED.
CONTINUE TRADITIONS, NO MATTER HOW SMALL
GO ON WITH YOUR LIFE, DON'T JUST STARE AT THE WALL
I MISS YOU ALL DEARLY, SO KEEP UP YOUR CHIN
UNTIL THE DAY COMES THAT WERE TOGETHER AGAIN.

There was also another poem that our dear friend Drema Akers shared with us as it came close to Christmas time, following Faye's death. It is as follows:

"Christmas in Heaven"

I see the countless Christmas Trees around the world below

with tiny lights like heavens stars reflecting on the snow.

The sight is so spectacular please wipe away that tear for I am spend-ing Christmas with Jesus Christ this year.

I hear the many Christmas songs that people hold so dear but the sound of music can't compare with the Christmas choir up here.

I have no words to tell you of the joy their voices bring for it is beyond description to hear the angels sing.

I know how much you miss me, I see the pain inside your heart for I am spending Christmas with Jesus Christ this year.

I can't tell you of the splendor or the peace here in this place.

Can you just imagine Christmas with our Savior, face to face?

I'll ask him to lift your spirit as I tell him of your love so then pray for one another as you lift your eyes above.

Please let your hearts be joyful and let your our spirit sing

For I am spending Christmas in heaven

and I'm walking with the King.

It will soon be three years since my wife passed away. There is a lady at the church, and her husband passed away about ten years ago. Her name is Barbara and she plays the piano at the church. The two of us go out to eat every once in a while. We enjoy talking to each other. We talk to each other about the problems we may have and our families. We are both Christians and we both know the laws of the Bible. I have a lot of respect for her and she said if she didn't trust me she wouldn't go anyplace with me. I am thankful she does trust me and that I have a good friend like her to talk to and go out to eat with. One night she and I took her mother out to have a cup of coffee, and her mother said Lawrence, I would like to go to Pigeon Forge Tennessee and see the Christmas lights. I asked her if she really wanted to go and she said yes, so, we all loaded up in my motor-home, along with my youngest daughter and we headed to the Smokey Mountains. We really had a good time. Barbara has a nice family. She and I had a cook out for both of our families along with some of our church friends, and their wives.

I am about to roll this ball of yarn up and if you by chance have read this, tell someone else and maybe they will get a kick out of this Good Ole Country Boy's life, but most of all look up to the Lord. He is looking down, he may have a smile for you, and may bless your little pea pickin' heart.